Government Reference Books

GOVERNMENT REFERENCE BOOKS 68/69

A Biennial Guide to
U.S. Government Publications

COMPILED BY

SALLY WYNKOOP

FIRST BIENNIAL EDITION 1970

LIBRARIES UNLIMITED, INC.

INTRODUCTION

Librarians have long been aware of the wealth of information available in government publications. Increasingly, schools, business, and industry are taking advantage of the material compiled and published by government agencies. In contrast to the growing interest in and use of government documents by the public, the development of bibliographic tools for quick access to information buried in the mountain of government publications has been slow and uncoordinated.

Government Reference Books is a new bibliographic tool aimed at providing continuing coverage of reference works published by the Government Printing Office. The first edition of this biennial is an annotated subject guide to over 600 titles published by the Government Printing Office during 1968 and 1969.

The United States government is the world's largest publisher. There were 17,443 entries in the 1969 *Monthly Catalog* alone. Although not all *Monthly Catalog* entries are Government Printing Office publications, this figure still does not reflect the great number of scientific and technical materials published by the Clearinghouse for Federal Scientific and Technical Information nor the many non-GPO publications issued by the various departments and agencies which never get listed in the *Monthly Catalog.*

There is no systematic attempt to review reference-type government publications in library periodicals. In March 1969 *Wilson Library Bulletin* began a monthly column by Frederic J. O'Hara entitled "Selected Government Publications—Reference Books and Other Worthwhile Titles." An average of 20 titles are discussed in each issue (or about 200 a year) but, as the column title suggests, not all are reference works nor are they necessarily recent publications. Joe Morehead's fine column, "A Mazeway Miscellany: U.S. Government Documents," in *RQ* is an informative and entertaining guide to both publications and activities of the federal government. It discusses recent publications of general interest but not all are reference works and only about 50 titles a year are included. Other periodicals make no attempt to include government documents in their reviewing services on a regular basis.

There are some bibliographies, such as Jackson's *Subject Guide to United States Government Publications*, which deal specifically with government documents. Each has its own criteria for inclusion but none deal exclusively with reference works and they are not always current. Many of the major retrospective bibliographies, such as Winchell's *Guide to Reference Books*, include government documents, but so selectively as to be only a token of what may be found. The new publication, *American Reference Books Annual*, does include current government documents, but again on a selective basis.

This comprehensive bibliography will be published biennially to keep librarians abreast of new and worthwhile government reference books. It will also constitute a permanent record of the important works in many different fields of interest.

The types of reference materials included are bibliographies, directories, indexes, dictionaries, statistical works, handbooks and guides, almanacs, catalogs of collections, and biographical directories. Entries are arranged under three broad areas: social sciences, science and engineering, and humanities, and are subdivided by some 100 specific subjects. Complete bibliographic citations are provided including price, LC Card number, if any, and Superintendent of Documents classification number. Descriptive annotations state purpose, scope, arrangement and details of coverage, as well as special features of each publication. The author-title-subject index facilitates alphabetical access to materials listed in the bibliography.

Two appendixes are included: The first discusses major bibliographic sources for locating current government documents and tells how to order publications found in those sources. Addresses and, in some cases, costs are included. The second appendix is a directory of federal government agencies which issue or publish the materials listed in the bibliography.

It is hoped that this biennial bibliography of government reference books will not only assist librarians in selecting materials for their collections but will also aid them in servicing government documents and filling patron requests. It should also be helpful as a reference aid for researchers, local, state and national officials, employees of federal agencies, educators, businessmen, labor officials and interested individuals.

TABLE OF CONTENTS

PART ONE

PART TWO

PART THREE

13

14

PART ONE

SOCIAL SCIENCES

SOCIAL SCIENCES

GENERAL WORKS

BIBLIOGRAPHIES

1.   U.S. Department of State. Office of External Research. **External Research, List of Current Social Science Research by Private Scholars and Academic Centers: Africa.** Washington, Department of State, 1968. 63 p. Issuing Agency. LC Card No. 53-61430. S 1.101:5.27

Bibliography of current social science research on Africa. Material is collected from individual scholars and academic institutions. Arranged by country and subject of research. Annotations are provided only if sent by the scholars and academic centers. No indexes. "Available to libraries, scholars and universities only."

2.   U.S. Department of State. Office of External Research. **External Research, List of Current Social Science Research by Private Scholars and Academic Centers: American Republics.** Washington, Department of State, 1968. 104 p. Issuing Agency. LC Card No. 53-61429. S 1.101:6.27

Bibliography of current social science research on Latin America. Material is collected from individual scholars and academic institutions. Arranged by country and subject of research. Annotations are provided only if sent by the scholars and academic centers. No indexes. "Available to libraries, scholars and universities only."

3.   U.S. Department of State. Office of External Research. **External Research, List of Current Social Science Research by Private Scholars and Academic Centers: Asia.** Washington, Department of State, 1968. 117 p. Issuing Agency. LC Card No. 68-60199. S 1.101:2.27

Bibliography of current social science research on Asia. Material is collected from individual scholars and academic institutions. Arranged by country and subject of research. Annotations are provided only if sent by the scholars and academic centers. No indexes. "Available to libraries, scholars and universities only."

4.   U.S. Department of State. Office of External Research. **External Research, List of Current Social Science Research by Private Scholars and Academic Centers: International Affairs.** Washington, Department of State, 1968. 104 p. Issuing Agency. LC Card No. 54-61701. S 1.101:7.27

Bibliography of current research on international affairs. Material is collected from individual scholars and academic institutions. Arranged by specific subject of research. Annotations are provided only if sent by the scholars and academic centers. No indexes. "Available to libraries, scholars, and universities only."

5.   U.S. Department of State. Office of External Research. **External Research, List of Current Social Science Research by Private Scholars and Academic Centers: Middle East.** Washington, Department of State, 1968. 25 p. Issuing Agency. LC Card No. 53-60845. S 1.101:4.27

Bibliography of current social science research on the Middle East. Material is collected from individual scholars and academic institutions. Arranged by country and subject of research. Annotations are provided only if sent by the scholars and academic centers. No indexes. "Available to libraries, scholars and universities only."

6.   U.S. Department of State. Office of External Research. **External Research, List of Current Social Science Research by Private Scholars and Academic Centers: USSR and Eastern Europe.** Washington, GPO, 1968. 60 p. Issuing Agency. LC Card No. 53-61425. S 1.101:1.27

Bibliography of current social science research on the USSR and Eastern Europe. Material is collected from individual scholars and academic institutions. Arranged by country and subject of research. Annotations are provided only if sent by the scholars and institutions. No indexes. Issued annually. "Available to libraries, scholars and universities only."

7.   U.S. Department of State. Office of External Research. **External Research, List of Current Social Science Research by Private Scholars and Academic Centers: Western Europe, Great Britain, and Canada.** Washington, Department of State, 1968. 105 p. Issuing Agency. LC Card No. 53-61426. S 1.101:3.27

Bibliography of current social science research on Western Europe, Great Britain, and Canada. Material is collected from individual scholars and academic institutions. Arranged by country and subject of research. Annotations are provided only if sent by scholars and academic centers. No indexes. "Available to libraries, scholars and universities only."

EDUCATION

GENERAL WORKS
BIBLIOGRAPHIES

8.   U.S. National Institutes of Health. **Educational Technology and the Teaching-Learning Process, A Selected Bibliography.** Prep. by Jeanne Saylor Berthold and Mary Alice Curran. Washington, National Institutes of Health, 1968. 63 p. Issuing Agency. LC Card No. 68-67053. FS 2.22/13: T22

   "This bibliography is intended to serve as an introduction to the literature on the teaching-learning process and on the various new approaches in the field of teaching technology." Primarily recent books and journal articles are included, arranged alphabetically under major subject headings. Not annotated or indexed.

9.   U.S. Office of Education. **Education, Literature of the Profession: Bibliography Based on Acquisitions of the Educational Materials Center from April 16, 1966 to December 31, 1968.** By Eunice Von Ende. Washington, GPO, 1969. 34 p. $0.45. LC Card No. 77-602722. FS 5.210:10060

   This bibliography on the literature of the education profession lists entries by subject under "Interpretation and Comment" or "Bibliographies and Directories." Many entries are annotated. Includes a list of periodicals with ordering information and a directory of publishers.

10.   U.S. Office of Education. **Office of Education Publications.** Washington, GPO, 1969 –. Semi-annual. $0.40. FS 5.211:11000-yr.- no.

   Issued to date: 11000-68 and 11000-69-1.

   Lists all publications issued during the year (or six month period). Arranged by type of educational specialty and then by OE numbers. Annotated. Not indexed.

11.   U.S. Office of Education. **Publications of the Office of Education.** Washington, GPO, 1968. 81 p. $0.45. LC Card No. HEW64-37. FS 5.211: 11000(F)

   Lists publications from the Office of Education which are currently available, regardless of publication date. Arranged by type of educational specialty. Within each category, arranged by OE number. Annotated with title index.

12.   U.S. Office of Education. **Reference Tools 1968-69; a Bibliography Based on Acquisitions of the Educational Materials Center from January 1968-July 1969.** Prep. by Caroline Stanley. Washington, GPO, 1969. 10 p. $0.25. FS 5.210:10063

Arranged by type of reference tool, e.g. encyclopedias, dictionaries, atlases, bibliographies and periodicals which might have reference value in elementary and secondary schools. Some annotations are provided. Not indexed.

DIRECTORIES

13.   U.S. Department of State. Advisory Council on the Arts. **Cultural Presentations USA, 1967-1968.** Washington, GPO, 1969. 78 p. Illus. $0.40. LC Card No. 62-60432. S 1.67:98

This report to the Congress and the public lists professional, academic and athletic programs by Americans on tour abroad. Includes photographs of the groups, tour schedules, audience statistics, and selected press reviews.

14.   U.S. Office of Education. **Directory of Consultants on Migrant Education.** Washington, Office of Education, 1969. 87 p. Issuing Agency. LC Card No. 77-603048. FS 5.2:M58/7

Contains national and state lists for migrant education programs under Title I, Elementary and Secondary Education Act, PL89-10, as amended.
"Lists consultants who are knowledgeable and available to help state and local educational agencies develop plans and approaches—short-range and long-range—to effectively educate these children of migratory agricultural workers." Alphabetically by state with names and addresses and areas of specialization. The national list is in a separate section.

15.   U.S. Office of Education. **Directory, State Departments of Education Personnel for Guidance and Personnel Services.** Washington, GPO, 1969. 28 p. Issuing Agency. LC Card No. HEW61-70. FS 5.225:25037-C

Lists names, addresses, titles and telephone numbers for state departments of education personnel alphabetically by state. Includes persons responsible for guidance, and counseling and testing as well as school psychological services when they are part of the same organizational unit.

16.   U.S. Office of Education. **Education Directory.** Washington, GPO, 1894/95— . Annual. LC Card No. E13-213. FS 5.25:yr./pts.

Published from 1895 to 1911 as a chapter of the report of the Commissioner of Education and continued from 1912 as a bulletin of the Office of Education. Annotations for Parts I and IV are based on the 1967/68 edition, for Parts II and III on the 1968-69 editions.

Part I: **State Governments**
Arranged alphabetically by states, listing principal people in state agencies dealing with elementary and secondary education, and vocational-technical education. Professional members of state education departments are included and other state service organizations are described. Professional members of state library extension agencies are also included.

Part II. **Public School Systems, 1968/69.** 1969. 205 p. $2.00

School districts of 300 or more pupils are included in this section, except those run by states or the federal government and those operated by colleges and universities. Arranged alphabetically by state and then by school system. Gives location of the superintendent, zip code, county name, enrollment and grade span. Also lists any administrative units for each state. Past issues listed church affiliated schools but this is no longer included.

Part III: **Higher Education, 1968/69.** 1969. 459 p. $4.25

"Lists institutions of higher education in the United States offering at least a two-year program of college-level studies in residence, submitting the information required for listing." Previous editions had accredition criteria for inclusion; now, a computer print-out enables all schools to be included with a symbol denoting accrediting agency, if any. Lists schools alphabetically within each state and lists the following information for each: address, control or affiliation, co-ed or not, calendar system, highest degree offered, type of program, enrollment and names and titles of administrative officials. Includes supplementary material such as a list of higher education associations, schools now listed under new names, and those in new locations.

Part IV: **Education Associations, 1967/68.** 1969. 141 p. $0.60

Lists associations alphabetically and for each it provides the address of headquarters, name and address of the chief officer, name and address of the secretary and title or titles of official periodical publications and the frequency. Divided into broad headings such as State Education Associations, and Foundations. Index by subjects with names of associations listed under each.

17. U.S. Office of Education. **Inventory of Federal Programs Involving Educational Activities Concerned with Improving International Understanding and Cooperation: An Interagency Survey Conducted for the Congress of the United States by the Department of Health, Education and Welfare.** Washington, GPO, 1969. 545 p. $4.75. LC Card No. 70-604405. FS 5.214:14142

Cites 159 programs authorized under 42 different acts of Congress, which include "educational activities aimed at improved international understanding and cooperation." Programs are listed under administrative agency of the U.S. government, with full description, legislative authority, purposes, amounts and sources of funds, methods of administration, and other relevant statistical information. Appendixes provide a summary of legislative authorities and an inventory chart.

18. U.S. Office of Education. **Public Advisory Committees.** Washington, GPO, 1968. 75 p. Issuing Agency. LC Card No. HEW68-121. FS 5.211:11019

A directory of 26 committees (e.g. Advisory Committee on Accreditation and Institutional Eligibility, and Advisory Council on College Library Resources), which act in some way to help carry out the programs and services of the Office of Education. Lists the legal authority (Executive Order or Public Law), the functions of the committees, how members are appointed, terms of office, compensation and travel expense authorization, number of members and a complete list of members with the addresses, positions, and expiration date of their memberships.

19.   U.S. Office of Education. Institute of International Studies. **Some Opportunities Abroad for Teachers, 1970-71; United States Government Grants Under the Fulbright-Hays Act.** Washington, GPO, 1969. 23 p. Issuing Agency. LC Card No. E53-47. FS 5.214:14047-71

Formerly called **Opportunities Abroad for Teachers Under the International Education and Cultural Exchange Program,** but changed with the 1969/70 edition. Its basic aim is to list opportunities available to U.S. teachers in foreign countries. Arranged alphabetically by country which has positions.

LAWS

20.   U.S. Senate. Committee on Labor and Public Welfare. Subcommittee on Education. **Education Legislation.** Washington, GPO, 1968. 53 p. Issuing Agency. Y 4.L11/2:Ed8/22/967/pt.11

Directory of 1,845 college Work-Study Programs authorized under Title I, Part C of the Economic Opportunity Act of 1964. Colleges and universities are arranged alphabetically within states. Names of college presidents, allocations, and estimated number of student awards are reported.

READING LISTS

21.   U.S. Library of Congress. **Children and Poetry: A Selective Annotated Bibliography.** Comp. by Virginia Haviland and William J. Smith. Washington, GPO, 1969. 67 p. Issuing Agency (Children's Book Section, General Reference and Bibliography Division). LC Card No. 70-603744. LC 1.12/2:P75

An annotated selective bibliography of poetry for children which includes rhyme and more serious poetry, old and new works, works in English and translations. Annotations often include selections from verses in the particular book and are both descriptive and evaluative.

22.   U.S. Library of Congress. **Children's Books, 1968, A List of Books for Preschool through Junior High School Age.** Comp. by Virginia Haviland and Lois Watt. Washington, GPO, 1969. 16 p. $0.15. LC Card No. 65-60014. LC 2.11:968

A listing of picture books, stories for older children, folklore, biography, poetry, plays, Bible stories, histories, and science books for children published in 1968. Annotated but not indexed.

23.   U.S. Office of Education. **Books Related to the Social Studies in Elementary and Secondary Schools: A Bibliography from the Educational Materials Center.** Comp. by Lois B. Watt and others. Washington, GPO, 1969. 27 p. $0.35. LC Card No. 72-605030. FS 5.231:31011

A selective annotated bibliography of the text and trade books received in the Center between January 1968 and May 1969 which were favorably reviewed in journals or found on basic lists. Part I, Juvenile Literature, is arranged by regions of the world. Part II is similarly arranged for adolescent literature. Includes 284 titles. Annotations are brief descriptions with grade span and code for fiction and folklore. Since only books receiving favorable reviews or listings are included, the citation to source would have been a useful inclusion.

24.   U.S. Office of Education. **Literature for Disadvantaged Children, A Bibliography.** From the Educational Materials Center, Division of Information Technology and Dissemination, Bureau of Research. Comp. by Lois B. Watt. Washington, GPO, 1968. 16 p. $0.20. LC Card No. 68-62995. FS 5.237:37019

Reprinted from a section of **The Education of Disadvantaged Children,** an Office of Education document published in a limited edition, in order to meet requests from teachers, librarians, and other educators. Includes books received in the Educational Materials Center from 1964 to 1966, with a new edition planned. Arranged by author under broad subject headings. Annotated. Grade levels given for all publications. Not indexed.

ELEMENTARY & SECONDARY EDUCATION

BIBLIOGRAPHIES

25.   U.S. National Agricultural Library. **School Lunches and Other School Feeding Programs, 1962-July 1967, List of Selected References.** Comp. by Betty B. Baxtresser. Washington, National Agricultural Library, 1968. 28 p. Library List No. 88. Issuing Agency. LC Card No. Agr68-161. A 17.17:88

Brings up to date Library Lists 26, 57, and 74, which are bibliographies on school lunches for the years 1925 through 1961. Includes "school lunches actually served at school, special school breakfasts, special summer lunch programs, Project Head Start feeding programs, and disaster feeding in which school lunch facilities were used." Excludes material on nutrition of children. Arranged by subjects. Not annotated. Indexed by authors and subjects.

DIRECTORIES

26.   U.S. Office of Education. **Directory: Public Elementary and Secondary Schools in Large School Districts; with Enrollment and Instructional Staff, By Race: Fall 1967.** Washington, GPO, 1969. 840 p. $7.25. LC Card No. 72-604076. FS 5.220:20121

"Single-time publication developed to meet a specific, timely need for information" about the racial composition of schools. Alphabetical by state and city. For each school, it tells grade span, number of pupils (total white, Negro and other) and instructional staff (total white, Negro and other).

27.   U.S. Office of Education. **Nonpublic School Directory, 1965-66; Elementary and Secondary Schools.** Washington, GPO, 1968. 269 p. $2.25. FS 5.220:20043-66

This edition includes, for the first time, elementary and secondary schools. Includes schools which responded to questionnaires sent out by the Office of Education. Lists names of independent or church affiliated secondary schools for the first time in a separate publication. Each school is listed under the state in which it is located with address, span of grades, years in school, accreditation (state/regional), number of teachers, enrollment and number of graduates in the past year. Excludes nonpublic schools which offer training in specific skills rather than in academic curriculum. Evening schools offering secondary education as well as schools for special or disadvantaged students are included. No indexes.

28.   U.S. Office of Education. Division of Compensatory Education. **Profiles of Quality Education.** Washington, GPO, 1968.   123 p. $1.25.   LC Card No. HEW68-131.   FS 5.237:37018

Describes 150 outstanding Title I ESEA (Elementary and Secondary Education Act) projects from across the U.S. "Each project has been designated by State Title I Coordinators as worthy of emulation. Each provides valuable assistance to the low-income children it serves." Includes various types of programs, such as preschool, integration, language arts, summers, parent participation. Specific programs are randomly arranged within their types. Gives description of each program, as well as place, starting date, cost, staff, participants and name and address of program director. Indexed by subjects and states.

29.   U.S. Office of Education. Research Bureau. **Regional Education Laboratories.**   Washington, GPO, 1968.   20 p.   Issuing Agency.   FS 5.212:12030

This is the Office of Education's first directory of laboratories funded by Title IV, Elementary and Secondary Education Act. Arranged alphabetically by official title, region and address. Includes director's name, immediate past position, length of time in present position, and number of professional staff members. Short descriptions of important programs are also provided.

STATISTICS

30.   U.S. Office of Education. **Fall 1968 Statistics of Public Elementary and Secondary Day Schools: Pupils, Teachers, Instruction Rooms, and Expenditures.**   By Richard H. Barr and Betty J. Foster.   Washington, GPO, 1969. 33 p. $0.45.   LC Card No. 65-9607.   FS 5.220:20007-68

Provides current data on the number of local school districts, enrollment by grade, high school graduates, teachers, instruction rooms, estimated expenditure, and average salaries of the staff. This data is given for each state and outlying area and for 14 of the largest cities.

31.   U.S. Office of Education. **Public School Finance Programs, 1968-69.** Washington, GPO, 1969.   335 p. $3.00.   FS 5.222:22002-69

"Sixth in a series of compendiums prepared by the U.S. Office of

Education in cooperation with the 50 States and Outlying Areas in order to provide a concise description of State systems of school support." Its primary purpose is to provide a "description of State funds transmitted to local agencies for the support of elementary and secondary education." Arranged alphabetically by state with programs detailed, authorizing legislation and statistical data.

32.   U.S. Office of Education. National Center for Educational Statistics. **Statistics of Local Public School Systems, 1967.** By Gerald Kahn and others. Washington, GPO, 1969. 101 p. $1.00. FS 5.220:20112-67

This continues the collection and dissemination of general basic statistics on local public school systems reported from 1871 to 1918 in the **Annual Report of the Commissioner of Education** and from 1918 to 1956 in the **Biennial Survey of Education in the United States** plus a series of annual studies on **Current Expenditures Per Pupil In Public School Systems** from 1918 to 1960.

The present report, planned for annual release, expands coverage from data on urban school systems only to include a representative sample of all types of local school systems. Contains three main parts: school systems, schools and pupils; instructional staff; and current expenditures. Includes numbers of school systems, enrollment, schools by grade span, size of schools, pupil-staff ratios and current expenditures per pupil.

HIGHER EDUCATION

DIRECTORIES

33.   U.S. Office of Education. **Directory of Counselor Educators, 1967-68.** Washington, GPO, 1968. 146 p. $1.00. LC Card No. HEW63-10. FS 5.225: 25036-B

Compiled first in 1962; revised January 1968. Defines a counselor educator as a person "who has been appointed for at least one academic year as a full-time member of a college or university faculty, recognized by the State Department of Education" and who either teaches or administers in the field of guidance education. Lists 1,119 counselor educators representing 372 institutions. First section is an alphabetical list of counselor educators by state and institution, with full title and telephone number for each. Second is a list of counselor educators alphabetically by name with address of the institution with which each is affiliated. Regional program officers of the Office of Education's nine areas are listed in the third section, followed by a list of state directors (for those who "wish to secure information about guidance certification requirements or other matters related to counselor education on a state-wide basis").

34.   U.S. Department of Labor. **Directory of Negro Colleges and Universities: Four Year Institutions Only.** Washington, GPO, 1969. 85 p. $1.00. LC Card No. 72-600862. L 1.54:N31/969

Alphabetical list of 85 colleges, universities, agricultural, mechanical and technical schools and one medical school. Data for each includes complete address and telephone number, names of executive staff members, current enrollment figures, degrees offered, number of degrees granted in the past three years, number expected to be granted in 1969, a description of the school, and affiliations (with accrediting and professional societies). Has a geographical index for locating schools in a particular state.

35.   U.S. Office of Education. **Eligible Institutions for the Guaranteed Student Loan Program under the Higher Education Act of 1965, as Amended April 30, 1969.** Washington, GPO, 1969. 143 p. Issuing Agency. LC Card No. HEW68-14. FS 5.2:In7/4

Lists eligible institutions for students who seek loans for higher education through the Guaranteed Loan program. Arranged alphabetically by states.

36.   U.S. Office of Education. **Experienced Teacher Fellowship Program.** Washington, Office of Education, 1968. 16 p. Issuing Agency. FS 5.258: 58010-69

"Discusses the graduate fellowships for experienced teachers and other school staff members that are authorized under the Higher Education Act of 1965 in order to help improve elementary and secondary education." Lists colleges and universities which sponsor programs leading to certification, masters degree, or other advanced degrees.

37.   U.S. Office of Education. **Institutions of Higher Education: Index by State and Congressional District.** By Leah W. Ramsey. Rev. ed. Washington, GPO, 1969. 45 p. Issuing Agency. LC Card No. 70-603893. FS 5.250:50060

Arranged by states and then Congressional districts, this directory lists the U.S. Representatives followed by the institutions of higher education in their districts, control (public or private), type of student body (male, female or coed), and the city in which each is located. Includes Canal Zone, Guam, Puerto Rico and the Virgin Islands.

38.   U.S. Office of Education. **National Defense Graduate Fellowships, Graduate Programs.** Washington, GPO, 1969. 52 p. Issuing Agency. LC Card No. HEW61-25. FS 5.255:55017-69-2

Outlines the purposes of the National Defense Graduate Fellowship Program, and generally describes the fellowships, and the allocation and awarding of them. The first section, "Approved Programs and Fellowship Allocations by State and Participating Institution," gives the number of fellowships and subjects for which they are awarded to each institution. Until the 1968/69 edition, there was a second part entitled "Approved Programs by Academic Discipline, with Name of Institution Offering Program." This is now omitted. Finally, there is a directory of participating institutions with approved programs for the year.

39. U.S. Office of Education. Bureau of Higher Education. **Search 1968.**
Washington, GPO, 1968. 62 p. $0.35. LC Card No. HEW68-135. FS 5.255:
55055

Purpose of the Educational Talent Search Program (as authorized by the
Higher Education Act of 1965) is to "identify and encourage young people of
exceptional financial need to complete high school and undertake or complete
postsecondary education and to inform these youths...of the [financial] opportunities available to them." The projects which work toward this objective are
described here, within geographic regions. Descriptions include the objectives,
services, source of funds, and any unique services. Index lists Talent Search
Programs alphabetically by sponsoring group.

STATISTICS

40a. U.S. Office of Education. **Financial Statistics of Institutions of Higher
Education: Current Funds, Revenues, and Expenditures, 1965-66.** By Paul F.
Mertins. Washington, GPO, 1969. 71 p. $0.70. FS 5.252:52010-66

40b. U.S. Office of Education. **Financial Statistics of Institutions of Higher
Education: Current Funds, Revenues, and Expenditures, 1966-67.** By Paul F.
Mertins. Washington, GPO, 1969. 81 p. $0.75. LC Card No. 79-603027.
FS 5.252:52010-67

The **Financial Statistics of Institutions of Higher Education** series includes
four parts. Three parts are listed here but the fourth, **Federal Funds 1965-66
and 1966-67** was not published during 1969. This part of the series presents
statistical information for the different aspects of revenues and expenditures
by geographic regions and then by states.

41a. U.S. Office of Education. **Financial Statistics of Institutions of Higher
Education: Property, 1965-66.** By Paul F. Mertins. Washington, GPO, 1969.
123 p. $1.25. LC Card No. E43-141. FS 5.252:52012-66

41b. U.S. Office of Education. **Financial Statistics of Institutions of Higher
Education: Property, 1966-67.** By Paul F. Mertins. Washington, GPO, 1969.
132 p. $1.25. FS 5.252:5012-67

Contains statistics on physical plant assets and indebtedness, endowment,
capital funds received and other aspects of property statistics for colleges and
universities. Includes a summary of the data.

42a. U.S. Office of Education. **Financial Statistics of Institutions of Higher
Education: Student Financial Aid, 1956-66.** By Paul F. Mertins. Washington,
GPO, 1969. 63 p. $0.65. FS 5.252:52011-66

42b. U.S. Office of Education. **Financial Statistics of Institutions of Higher
Education: Student Financial Aid, 1966-67.** By Paul F. Mertins. Washington,
GPO, 1969. 66 p. $0.65. LC Card No. 74-603066. FS 5.252:52011-67

This is a compendium of statistics on the types and amounts of student financial aid awarded at colleges and universities, by geographic regions and states.

43a. U.S. Office of Education. **Library Statistics of Colleges and Universities: Data for Individual Institutions, Fall, 1967.** Washington, GPO, 1969. 346 p. $2.50. LC Card No. 75-603026. FS 5.215:15023-67

Contains data on libraries of 2157 separate institutions and five joint libraries. The report is part of a series on general management data for libraries. The six tables cover operating expenditures 1966-67; enrollment and staff; holdings; square footage; indexes for expenditures, holdings, staff and funds; salaries. This issue includes for the first time percentage breakdowns of holdings and acquisitions by subject areas.

43b. U.S. Office of Education. **Library Statistics of Colleges and Universities: Data for Individual Institutions, Fall, 1968.** By Joel Williams. Washington, GPO, 1969. 172 p. $1.75.

Similar to above with data on 1841 individual libraries and seven joint libraries. Five tables cover holdings, 1967-68; actual expenditures, 1967-68; budgeted expenditures, 1967-68; staff and hours; and salary.

RESEARCH

DIRECTORIES

44. U.S. Office of Education. **Directory of Educational Information Centers.** Washington, GPO, 1969. 118 p. $1.25. LC Card No. 75-603574. FS 5.212:12042

This directory is a "listing of information centers offering services to educators in communities throughout the United States." Centers are listed by state and city with the following information given for each: (1) name and address, (2) head or director of the center and title, (3) telephone number, (4) founding date, (5) project number, (6) sponsor, (7) services offered and publications, (8) users or service limitations, and (9) holdings. Indexed by subject.

45. U.S. Office of Education. **Directory of Research in Social Studies/Social Sciences: Projects in the Teaching of Social Studies/Social Sciences and Related Disciplines Funded by the Bureau of Research.** Prep. by Anna R. Barrett and George S. Carnett. Washington, GPO, 1969. 27 p. $0.40. LC Card No. 72-605408. HE 5.231:31010

This is a useful directory for researchers, administrators, cirriculum directors, professional organizations and social studies teachers and is designed to keep them "abreast of current trends in the social and behavioral sciences with the objective of meeting the curriculum needs of the educational community." The first section lists projects by name of the investigator with title, Bureau of Research number, ERIC report number or ERIC project number. The second section lists investigators by discipline and the third lists projects closely related to the social sciences/social studies.

46. U.S. Office of Education. **Pacesetters in Innovation, v. 3, Fiscal Year 1968.** Washington, GPO, 1969. 311 p. $2.50. LC Card No. 71-601063. FS 5.220:20103-69.

Developed in cooperation with the Bureau of Research through the services of the Educational Resources Information Center (ERIC). PACE, the acronym for Projects to Advance Creativity in Education, was authorized under Title III of the Elementary and Secondary Education Act of 1965 to challenge educators to seek imaginative ways of making education more relevant to our society. Each volume of this series is a compilation of planning and operational grants for these projects awarded during the fiscal year. Two basic formats used are indexes and resumes. Indexes by subject, local education agency and project number, all of which are keyed to the accession numbers of the resumes. Resumes are arranged by accession numbers and include a detailed abstract of each project.

47. U.S. Office of Education. **Pacesetters in Innovation; Cumulative Issues of All Projects in Operation as of February 1969.** Washington, GPO, 1969. 584 p. $5.00. HE 5.220:20103-69

Provides information on Projects of Advance Creativity in Education (PACE) which were approved during fiscal years 1966-69, and were still in operation as of February 1969.

THESAURI

48. U.S. Office of Education. **Thesaurus of ERIC Descriptors (with Bibliography).** 2nd ed. Washington, GPO, 1969. 289 p. $3.25. LC Card No. HEW68-46. FS 5.212:12031-69

"An information retrieval thesaurus is a term-association list structured to enable indexers and subject analysts to describe the subject information of a document to a desired level of specificity at input, and to permit searchers to describe in mutually precise terms the information required at output. A thesaurus therefore serves as an authority list and as a device to bring into coincidence the language of documents and the language of questions." This thesaurus is used as an "authority for storing, searching and disseminating educational information." It should be consulted when using **Research in Education** (the monthly ERIC abstract journal). Descriptors are in bold face type with synonyms listed under each.

EARLY CHILDHOOD

BIBLIOGRAPHIES

49. U.S. Department of Health, Education and Welfare. **Bibliography on Early Childhood.** Washington, GPO, 1969. 16 p. Issuing Agency. LC Card No. 74-603693. FS 1.18:C43

This brief bibliography on early childhood cites publications alphabetically by author in sections for books or pamphlets and reprints. No annotations or index.

ADULT EDUCATION

BIBLIOGRAPHIES

50.   U.S. Office of Education. **Adult Basic Education; A Bibliography from the Educational Materials Center.** Comp. by Lois B. Watt and Sidney E. Murphy. Washington, GPO, 1968. 14 p. $0.30. LC Card No. HEW68-157. FS 5.214:14031-41

A bibliography of publications on teaching adults the "first essential skills of reading, writing, arithmetic, community living and citizenship." Lists all publications on these subjects which are in the Educational Materials Center. Includes teachers' resources in one section and students' texts in another. Most entries are annotated.

DIRECTORIES

51.   U.S. Women's Bureau. **Continuing Education Programs and Services for Women.** Compiled by Jean Wells. Washington, GPO, 1968. 104 p. $0.40. LC Card No. 68-62082. L 13.19:10/2

Provides a list of special educational programs for women and background information which explains to educators women's interest in and need for special programs. Schools with special programs for women are listed alphabetically by states. Includes "selected readings" on the subject and a list of schools which received federal funds for continuing education programs.

SPECIAL EDUCATION

BIBLIOGRAPHIES

52.   U.S. Office of Education. **Books Related to Compensatory Education.** Comp. by Lois B. Watt, Myra H. Thomas and Eunice Von Ende. Washington, GPO, 1969. 46 p. $0.50. LC Card No. 70-604358. FS 5.237:37045

A listing of books related to compensatory education which were received in the Office of Education's Educational Materials Center. Includes elementary and secondary school textbooks, juvenile literature and professional resources. Grade levels are given for the textbooks and juvenile literature as are symbols which indicate the major interest of the book (e.g. urban life, minority groups). Entries are descriptively annotated.

DIRECTORIES

53.   U.S. Office of Education. Bureau of Education for the Handicapped. Division of Training Programs. **Scholarship Program.** Washington, GPO, 1968. 45 p. Issuing Agency. FS 5.235:35059-D

Explains the program, its purpose and different types, and application procedures. Lists institutions and state educational agencies which participate in the program alphabetically by state. Abbreviations by the name of each institution explain the areas of the handicapped for which scholarships are offered.

VOCATIONAL EDUCATION

DIRECTORIES

54.   U.S. Office of Education. **Directory of Schools Offering Technical Education Programs Under Title III of the George-Barden Act and the Vocational Education Act of 1963.** Washington, Office of Education, 1968. 108 p. Issuing Agency. LC Card No. HEW68-118. FS 5.2:D62/2

Both Title III of the George-Barden Act and the Vocational Education Act of 1963 call for preparatory programs for pre-employment training. Prepared to "provide information regarding technical education programs to vocational educators, employers, and cooperating agencies." Contains names of schools and their locations and types of programs conducted. Arranged by states. Not indexed.

55.   U.S. Rehabilitation Services Administration. **Directory of State Divisions of Vocational Rehabilitation.** Washington, GPO, 1968. 96 p. Free. LC Card No. 68-60527. FS 17.102:St2/968

Arranged alphabetically by state listing name and address of state department of vocational rehabilitation, divisional supervisors and jurisdictions, and district supervisors and addresses.

Formerly called **Directory of State Divisions of Vocational Rehabilitation and State Agencies for the Blind,** (FS 13.202:St2/3/yr.).

RECREATION

BIBLIOGRAPHIES

56.   U.S. Bureau of Outdoor Recreation. **Index to Selected Outdoor Recreation Literature.** Washington, GPO, 1967– . Semiannual. $1.25. LC Card No. 68-60814. I 66.15:L71/vol.

Books and periodical articles are arranged by citation numbers giving full bibliographic information and a list of key words for each citation. There is approximately a year and a half delay between date of the publication and inclusion in this index, e.g. volume 4 published in November 1969 indexes materials published in the first half of 1968. Three separate indexes are necessary for use of this index: The subject index contains key words arranged alphabetically; the name index is to authors, editors, and corporate bodies; and a geographic index. All three indexes refer to citation numbers. Includes two valuable appendixes: (1) a list of periodicals from which articles have been cited; and (2) a list of books, documents, hearings, speeches, theses and dissertations, and bibliographies and directories cited. Volume one covers all 1966 publications; volume two includes those published during the first half of 1967, and volume three, the second half of 1967.

DIRECTORIES

57.   U.S. Bureau of Outdoor Recreation. **Guides to Outdoor Recreation Areas and Facilities.** Washington, GPO, 1968. 120 p. $0.40. I 66.15:G94/968

Compiled as a reference guide, this book lists sources of various publications of interest to those seeking information on outdoor recreation areas and facilities. Listed in three sections—National, Regional and State—with cross references for camping, canoeing, fishing and hunting.

58.   U.S. Bureau of Outdoor Recreation. **Federal Outdoor Recreation Programs.** Washington, GPO, 1968. 244 p. $1.75. LC Card No. 68-61966. I 66.2:P94

Prepared as part of the Outdoor Recreation Bureau's responsibility to "formulate and maintain a comprehensive nationwide outdoor recreation plan." First section is arranged by departments of the federal government, subdivided by their agencies and bureaus, which have outdoor recreation responsibilities. The functions of the agencies are summarized in this part with their specific outdoor recreation programs listed and cross-referenced to the detailed descriptions in the second section. Two indexes are provided: Index A is a "cross-reference chart" to programs (arranged alphabetically) showing type of program, supervising agency, and page number of the detailed description in Part B. Index B is an alphabetical listing of the federal agencies and bureaus which have outdoor recreation programs with page references to Part A.

59.   U.S. Bureau of Outdoor Recreation. **Outdoor Recreation Action.** Washington, GPO, 1966— . Quarterly. $2.00/yr. LC Card No. 67-60945. I 66.17: nos.

This series is a "forum for the reporting of private, local, State and Federal actions in the areas of outdoor recreation and natural beauty." Divided into broad classes such as "financing outdoor recreation," "technical assistance and education," and "organization and administration," with cross references from types of outdoor recreation action such as "fish and wildlife action." Gives a summary of action taken by federal, state, and local governments and private organizations. Indexed by states, federal government agencies and private organizations.

60.   U.S. Bureau of Outdoor Recreation. **Private Assistance in Outdoor Recreation; Directory of Organizations Providing Aid to Individuals and Public Groups.** Washington, GPO, 1968. 68 p. $0.30. LC Card No. 68-61218. I 66.2:D62/2/968

A selective listing of organizations which provide inexpensive "publications and other aids to the planning, development, and operation of outdoor recreation areas." Includes nonprofit professional societies and national organizations. Arranged alphabetically by specific type of recreation (e.g. archery, fishing, picnicking) with the concerned groups and their publications within these subjects. Gives a brief statement of policy for each organization, and a very brief annotation for each publication (including price and frequency). "The Bureau of Outdoor Recreation does not endorse or recommend these organizations, assistance provided, or publications over others not listed." An earlier edition (1966) is entitled **A Directory of Private Organizations Providing Assistance in Outdoor Recreation to Individuals, Organizations and Public Groups.**

61.   U.S. National Park Service. **National Parks and Landmarks.** Washington, GPO, 1968. 127 p. Illus. $0.55. LC Card No. 49-45754. I 29.66:968

Gives name, address, acreage and outstanding characteristics for each of the national parks, monuments, battlefields, cemeteries, historic sites, memorials, parkways, seashores, and recreation areas. Arranged alphabetically within each section by name of the area. Indexed.

SPORTS & HOBBIES

62.   U.S. Fish and Wildlife Service. **Duck Stamp Data.** Washington, GPO, 1969. 48 p. Illus. $0.30. I 49.4:111/5

A handy source for stamp collectors, hunters and conservationists. Provides a brief history of the federal duck stamp since the enactment of the Migratory Bird Hunting Stamp Act in 1934. Includes illustrations of the 36 duck stamps issued from 1934/35 to 1969/70, with information regarding the species featured, design, artist and pertinent philatelic data for each.

COMMUNICATIONS

MASS MEDIA

63a. U.S. President. Foreign Broadcast Information Service. **Broadcasting Stations of the World, 1969: Part 1, Amplitude Modulation Broadcasting Stations According to Country and City.** Washington, GPO, 1969. 242 p. $1.75. LC Card No. 47-32798. PrEx 7.9:969/pt.1

63b. U.S. President. Foreign Broadcast Information Service. **Broadcasting Stations of the World, 1969: Part 2, Amplitude Modulation Broadcasting Stations According to Frequency.** Washington, GPO, 1969. 248 p. $1.75. LC Card No. 47-32798. PrEx 7.9:969/pt.2

63c. U.S. President. Foreign Broadcast Information Service. **Broadcasting Stations of the World, 1969: Part 3, Frequency Modulation Broadcasting Stations.** Washington, GPO, 1969. 190 p. $1.50. LC Card No. 47-32798. PrEx 7.9:969/pt.3

63d. U.S. President. Foreign Broadcast Information Service. **Broadcasting Stations of the World, 1969: Part 4, Television Stations.** Washington, GPO, 1969. 329 p. $2.50. LC Card No. 47-32798. PrEx 7.9:969/pt.4

This annual publication lists all known radio and television stations except those which broadcast in the United States on domestic channels.

POSTAL GUIDES

64. U.S. Post Office Department. **Directory of Post Offices.** Washington, GPO, 1969. 485 p. $4.25. LC Card No. 55-61389. P 1.10/4:969

Lists post offices by state and name, with ZIP codes. Revised annually.

65. U.S. Post Office Department. **National ZIP Code Directory, 1969-70.** Washington, GPO, 1969. 1695 p. $10.50. LC Card No. 66-60919. P 1.10/8: 969

This official directory lists every postal delivery unit alphabetically by post office under state. Appendixes after state sections list ZIP codes for street addresses in larger cities.

SOCIOLOGY & SOCIAL CONDITIONS

SOCIAL WORK
BIBLIOGRAPHIES

66. U.S. Children's Bureau. **Good References on Day Care.** Washington,

Children's Bureau, 1968. 22 p. Free. LC Card No. HEW 68-119. FS 17.212: D33

Lists books and journal articles on day care center guides and standards, health and nutrition, parental involvement, administration and other aspects of day care center supervision. Provides address and cost of books listed. Annotated.

DIRECTORIES

67.   U.S. Department of Health, Education and Welfare. **Catalog of HEW Assistance Providing Financial Support and Services to State, Communities, Organizations, and Individuals.** Washington, GPO, 1969. 762 p. $5.50. LC Card No. 78-604100. FS 1.6/6:969

Arranged by type of assistance under the administrative agency of the Department of Health, Education and Welfare, this includes authorizing statute, administrator, program description, eligibility requirement, appropriations, Washington and local addresses, and other pertinent information for each program. Indexed by program subjects.

68.   U.S. Department of Health, Education and Welfare. Division of State Merit Systems. **Directory of State Merit Systems.** Washington, HEW, 1968. 31 p. Issuing Agency. LC Card No. 57-61886. FS 1.2:M54/968

"Covers the State merit systems serving the State and local agencies receiving Federal grants-in-aid and the Statewide civil service systems whose services include such State agencies. The multiple county merit systems covering local welfare, health, and civil defense personnel are also listed." State merit systems are defined as consisting of "systems which began as or have become Statewide civil service systems covering State agencies generally, and systems established primarily for the grants-in-aid programs." Arranged alphabetically by state listing the state board and agencies it services, and the personnel in charge of merit systems.

69.   U.S. Volunteers in Service to America. **VISTA Fact Book.** Washington, GPO, 1969. 12 issues. Issuing Agency. LC Card No. 67-62746. PrEx 10.21: 969

Compiled to provide current information on VISTA volunteers and projects. Lists all active projects including names of project contacts along with addresses and telephone numbers of local sponsors. It is divided by state and then by type of project (i.e. rural, urban, Indian, migrant, Job Corps, and mental health). Also contains a brief description of the work done by the volunteers.

70.   U.S. Women's Bureau. **Federal Funds for Day Care Projects.** Washington, Department of Labor, 1969. 73 p. Issuing Agency. LC Card No. 76-601339. L 13.2:D33/2/969

Lists government agencies which provide funds for day care centers, with authorization, eligibility requirements, funds, procedures for reviewing applications and sources of further information given for each.

STATISTICS

71.   U.S. National Center for Social Statistics. **Child Welfare Statistics, 1968.**
Washington, GPO, 1969. 45 p. Issuing Agency. FS 17.638:968

Reports statistics for the United States and each state on children receiving services from public and voluntary child welfare agencies and institutions, facilities for day care and foster care of children, personnel employed in public child welfare agencies and those granted educational leave, and expenditures for public child welfare services.

SOCIAL CONDITIONS

BIBLIOGRAPHIES

72.   U.S. Children's Bureau. **Selected References for Social Workers on Family Planning; An Annotated List.** Comp. by Mary E. Watts. Washington, GPO, 1968. 23 p. $0.25. LC Card No. HEW 68-41. FS 17.212:F21

Lists books and journal articles under the following headings: general, studies of attitudes about family planning, examples of family planning services, social work references, and others. Complete citations, descriptive annotations. Not indexed.

73.   U.S. Economic Research Service. **The Poor: A Selected Bibliography.**
By Peter R. Maida and John L. McCoy. Washington, GPO, 1969. 56 p. $0.60.
LC Card No. 70-602234. A1.38:1145

"A selected compilation of literature dealing with aspects of poverty in the United States." Includes publications in the fields of psychology, sociology, anthropology, demography, economics, and physical and mental health. Citations are in alphabetical order under major subject categories with no annotations. Author index.

74.   U.S. National Clearinghouse for Mental Health Information. **International Family Planning, 1966-68, a Bibliography.** By David L. Kasdon. Washington, GPO, 1969. 62 p. $0.35. LC Card No. 73-604079. FS 2.22/13:F21/2

Contains 217 citations and abstracts listed alphabetically by author with indexes by subjects and geographic regions. Includes books and journal articles published in the United States and abroad, and was published in order to help underdeveloped countries which are setting up their own population control programs. Covers 1966 to 1968 with "reasonable degree of comprehensiveness." Earlier publications were cited in another work entitled **Bibliography of Fertility Control** (edited by Christopher Tietze). Includes a list of journals fully covered in the bibliography.

75.   U.S. Social and Rehabilitation Service. **Poor People at Work: An Annotated Bibliography on Semi-Professionals in Education, Health and Welfare**

Services. By Linda I. Millman and Catherine S. Chilman. Washington, Social and Rehabilitation Service, 1969. 40 p. Issuing Agency. LC Card No. 79-602342. FS 17.17:P79

This bibliography includes "most of what has been written . . . in the professional literature and official reports in the past five years" concerning poor people employed as semi-professionals in human service occupations and participating in program planning in these fields and was prepared as an aid to professional personnel. It is arranged alphabetically under broad subject categories with descriptive annotations. One appendix contains a selective listing of sources which regularly feature articles on this subject, and another lists research centers devoted to developing, collecting or disseminating information in this field.

DIRECTORIES

76. U.S. Senate. Committee on Government Operations. **Staff Study of Campus Riots and Disorders, October 1967—May 1969.** Prep. by Daniel Harris and Joseph Honcharik. Washington, GPO, 1969. 52 p. Issuing Agency. LC Card No. 76-602490. Y 4.G74/6:R47/3

Gives a chronological listing of disturbances with name of institution, location, president, enrollment, and pertinent remarks for each. Includes an alphabetical listing by name of college or university.

77. U.S. Senate. Committee on Government Operations. Permanent Subcommittee on Investigations. **Staff Study of Major Riots and Civil Disorders, 1965 through July 31, 1968.** Prep. by Robert E. Dunne and B. Crichton Jones. Washington, GPO, 1968. 19 p. Issuing Agency. LC Card No. 72-60054. Y 4.G74/6:R47/2

A listing of major civil disorders in U.S. cities. Criteria for inclusion were that each riot have had two or more of the following: 2 or more injuries, sniping, looting, 20 or more fires, 50 or more arrests. Information was obtained from mayors of cities and reviewing news publications. Lists 166 cities which had riots chronologically by year and then alphabetically. Information for each includes: population, percent Negro population, injuries, types of crime, number of arrests, and estimated property damage. Not indexed.

RACE RELATIONS

BIBLIOGRAPHIES

78. U.S. Department of Housing and Urban Development. **Equal Opportunity; Bibliography of Research on Equal Opportunity in Housing.** Comp. by the Department of Housing and Urban Development Library. Washington, GPO, 1969. 24 p. $0.30. HH 1.28:86

This bibliography contains "a representative sampling of published studies on equal opportunity in housing, . . . and is designed as a source of ideas and materials which might stimulate and assist in solving problems of fair housing." Lists publications under headings such as economic aspects, sociological studies, community action process and research needs and methodology. Indexed by authors.

79.   U.S. Inter-Agency Committee on Mexican American Affairs. **The Mexican American: A New Focus on Opportunity, A Guide to Materials Relating to Persons of Mexican American Heritage in the United States.** Washington, Inter-Agency Committee on Mexican American Affairs, 1969. 186 p. Issuing Agency. LC Card No. 73-601854. Y 3.In8/23:10/M41

An unannotated list arranged alphabetically under categories: books; reports, hearings and proceedings; periodical literature; listing of currently published periodicals; dissertations; bibliographies; a-v materials; plus a listing of U.S. producers or distributors of Spanish language radio and television stations. The titles listed in the section on audio-visual materials are very briefly annotated. Periodical literature is arranged by title of periodical followed by an alphabetical author list of articles.

80.   U.S. Social Security Administration. **Not Just Some of Us: A Limited Bibliography on Minority Group Relations.** Washington, Social Security Administration, 1968. 31 p. Issuing Agency. LC Card No. HEW 68-64. FS 3.38:M66

Published in an "effort to provide a source book of information and readings in minority group relations" with the intention of "increasing knowledge and deepening understanding." Arranged by broad subjects; short annotations. Contains a separate list of reference materials. Not indexed.

81.   U.S. Veteran's Administration. **We Hold These Truths.** Prep. by Rosemary D. Reid. Washington, GPO, 1969. 31 p. Issuing Agency. LC Card No. 70-603223. VA 1.20/3:10-7

This bibliography lists books, pamphlets and other materials that "bear on the struggle for equality in station and in opportunity and on the philosophies and circumstances to which it is pertinent." Materials are listed alphabetically by author under the following headings: prejudice, minorities, employment, the Negro, questions, answers, study guides, and pamphlets and short articles.

RURAL LIFE

BIBLIOGRAPHIES

82.   U.S. Economic Research Service. **Selected Bibliography on Special Districts and Authorities in the United States, Annotated.** By Benjamin Novak. Washington, GPO, 1968. 57 p. $0.40. LC Card No. Agr68-181. A 1.38:1087

Special districts are defined as "essentially rural developments" which were set up as the organizational and governmental solution to rural problems such as irrigation, conservation, flood prevention, etc. They are "public corporate entities which exist outside the regular structure of government." This bibliography is concerned only with special districts and authorities created by state legislation. The first section lists journal articles, followed by books, studies and reports, and then government publications (including federal, state, and local). All entries are annotated. Includes in a separate chapter, bibliographies on the subject. Lists addresses of many publishers of relevant materials. Indexes by subjects, authors and states.

83.　U.S. National Agricultural Library. **Non-Urban Patterns of Land Utilization, 1963-68.** Comp. by Betty Baxtresser. Washington, National Agricultural Library, 1968. 39 p. (Library List No. 93). Issuing Agency. LC Card No. Agr68-310. A 17.17:93

Presents selected references on "current and projected patterns of non-urban land utilization and the effects of these patterns on rural growth, transportation, land values, public lands, forest resources, natural resource conservation, and regional planning." Includes periodical literature published from January 1965 through May 1968 and books from 1963 to May 1968. Arranged by broad subjects with author and subject indexes.

84.　U.S. Rural Electrification Administration. **Current REA Publications.** Washington, REA, 1969. 39 p. Issuing Agency. A 68.3:Ind/969

Lists current publications of the Rural Electrification Administration's Rural Telephone Program. Subject index.

DIRECTORIES

85.　U.S. Rural Community Development Service. **Legislative Summary of Federal Programs Available to Assist Rural Americans.** Washington, Department of Agriculture, 1968. 99 p. Issuing Agency. LC Card No. 68-157. A 97.2:L52

Directory of laws passed during the 90th Congress, 1st Session which pertain to the improvement of rural conditions in the United States. Lists laws in part one by type of emphasis (e.g. economic development, education, health and welfare). Part two lists laws by number. A final section contains the same information for laws passed in the 87th—89th Congresses.

URBAN LIFE

BIBLIOGRAPHIES

86.　U.S. Department of Housing and Urban Development. **Selected Information Sources for Urban Specialists.** Prep. by the HUD Clearinghouse Service. Washington, GPO, 1969. 43 p. $0.50. LC Card No. 78-604344. HH 1.35:D/1

Primarily a directory of organizations and services available to planners, government officials, and others working in urban and urban related fields, this publication includes basic information about referral, reference, abstracting and document reproducing services that are "designed to serve a nationwide clientele." Lists sources or services under urban related headings such as education, law enforcement, population, employment and economic statistics or type of service such as information centers. Provides names, locations, directors, purposes, characteristics and general directions for using each system.

87.   U.S. Department of Housing and Urban Development. **Urban Outlook; a Selected Bibliography of Films, Filmstrips, Slides, and Audiotapes.** Washington, GPO, 1969. 38 p. $0.45. LC Card No. 74-603196. HH 1.28:95 (PB-178 811)

88.   U.S. National Institute of Mental Health. **Bibliography on the Urban Crisis; the Behavioral, Psychological and Sociological Aspects of Urban Crisis.** By Jon K. Meyer. Washington, GPO, 1969. 452 p. $3.75. LC Card No. 73-605766. HE 20.2417:Ur1

This bibliography provides a comprehensive and extensive listing of behavioral, psychological and sociological literature, both academic and popular, on various aspects of life in our cities and on the causes, effects, and responses to urban disorders. Emphasis was placed on materials published from 1954 to 1968, but earlier materials are also represented. Citations are listed first under one of 10 broad subject categories, second by year of publication and then alphabetically by author with entry numbers for each. Detailed author and subject indexes refer to entry numbers.

DIRECTORIES

89.   U.S. Department of Health, Education and Welfare. **HEW Cities Handbook.** Washington, GPO, 1969. 64 p. $0.50. FS 1.6/3:C49/969

"Designed to give local, state and Federal officials and planners a thumbnail guide to programs funded by the Department of Health, Education and Welfare." Programs are listed under the headings of health, education and social services. Directory lists the type of assistance, legislative authorization, appropriation amount, purpose, eligibility requirements, and where to write for further information.

YOUTH

BIBLIOGRAPHIES

90.   U.S. Children's Bureau. **Publications of the Children's Bureau.** Washington, GPO, 1969. 35 p. Issuing Agency. LC Card No. HEW 61-14. FS 17.212:P96/969

Lists all publications which are available for distribution, regardless of year published. Arranged under specific areas of concern (e.g. juvenile delinquency, child health). One alphabetical index to subjects and titles.

CRIMINOLOGY

BIBLIOGRAPHIES

91.   U.S. Children's Bureau. **The Prevention of Juvenile Delinquency; A Selected, Annotated Bibliography.** Washington, GPO, 1968. 15 p. $0.30. FS 17.212:J98

An alphabetical listing of 29 books or journal articles about prevention of juvenile delinquency, which can "serve to introduce concerned citizens, students, and others to recent thinking and developments in the field."

ANTHROPOLOGY & ETHNOLOGY

AMERICAN INDIANS

GENERAL WORKS

92.   U.S. Bureau of Indian Affairs. **American Indian Calendar.** Washington, GPO, 1969. 78 p. $0.45. I 20.2:C12/1/969

   A handy guide for tourists and those interested in Indian ceremonies, dances, feasts, and celebrations. Arranged first by states and then dates.

BIBLIOGRAPHIES

93.   U.S. Bureau of Indian Affairs. **Economic Development of American Indians and Eskimos, 1930—1967: A Bibliography.** By Marjorie P. Snodgrass. Washington, GPO, 1969. 263 p. $2.00. LC Card No. 79-601798. I 20.48: Ec7/930-67

   "This bibliography is a unique attempt to bring together in one place as much valuable information as possible on the economic development of the American Indians and Eskimos." Includes materials published in the United States from 1930 through 1967 and many unpublished works. Arranged alphabetically by author under 14 subject areas. Not annotated. Includes a reservation index and an appendix of Bureau field offices.

94.   U.S. Library of Congress. **Folklore of the North American Indians; an Annotated Bibliography.** Comp. by Judith C. Ullom. Washington, GPO, 1969. 126 p. Illus. $2.25. LC Card No. 70-601462. LC 2.2:In25

   Selective bibliography of the recorded folklore of North American Indians. Arranged by eleven culture areas, including Eskimo. Within each area are listed first the source books followed by editions for children. A section of general background information includes an annotated bibliography of folklore studies, anthologies, children's anthologies, bibliographies, and indexes. Indexed by subjects, authors and titles.

DIRECTORIES

95.   U.S. Bureau of Indian Affairs. **Field Office Addresses.** Washington, GPO, 1968. 6 p. Issuing Agency. I 20.38:968-4

   Lists 76 field offices in 25 states and principal tribes within the jurisdiction of each office. Addresses are included for the offices. Indian employment assistance offices with addresses supplement the directory.

LAW

BIBLIOGRAPHIES

96a. U.S. Children's Bureau. **Legal Bibliography for Juvenile and Family Courts.** By William H. Sheridan and Alice B. Freer. Washington, GPO, 1966. 46 p. $0.35. LC Card No. HEW 66-96. FS 14.112:L52

96b. U.S. Children's Bureau. **Legal Bibliography for Juvenile and Family Courts. Supplement 1.** Washington, GPO, 1967. 34 p. $0.30.

96c. U.S. Children's Bureau. **Legal Bibliography for Juvenile and Family Courts. Supplement 2.** Washington, GPO, 1968. 38 p. $0.50.

Designed for use by "judges, probation officers, law enforcement personnel, counsel, and other professional persons in the field of delinquency and the law." Cites journal articles and specific cases. Arranged alphabetically in each chapter. Chapters on specific subjects. No indexes.

INDEXES

97. U.S. Library of Congress. Legislative Reference Service. **Digest of General Bills and Resolutions, 91st Congress, 1st Session.** Washington, GPO, 1969. $14.00/set of 2 volumes; $35.00/session of Congress. LC 14.6:91/1

The **Digest** was first prepared for the 2nd Session of the 74th Congress and has been prepared for all subsequent Congresses. Its purpose is to furnish a brief summary of essential features of public bills and resolutions and changes made therein during the legislative process. It also indicates committee action, floor action taken by either body of Congress, enactments, and includes a subject and author index. The **Digest** is usually published during each session in five or more cumulative issues with bi-weekly supplements as needed, and a final edition at the end of each session. The cumulative issues are divided into five parts: Part I, Status of Measures Receiving Action; Part II, Public Laws; Part III, Digests of Public General Bills and Resolutions; Part IV, Author (i.e. sponsor) index; and Part V, Subject-matter index.

CIVIL RIGHTS

98. U.S. Commission on Civil Rights. **Catalog of Publications.** Washington, Civil Rights Commission, 1969. 15 p. Issuing Agency. CR 1.9:C28/969

99. U.S. Commission on Civil Rights. Clearinghouse. **Civil Rights Directory.** Washington, GPO, 1968. 168 p. Issuing Agency. LC Card No. 68-67294. CR 1.10:15

Consists of four sections: Section one, "officials of 38 federal agencies who are responsible for monitoring, administering, coordinating, and enforcing various aspects of equal opportunity laws and policies." Arranged by department and agency with titles and telephone numbers for each person, plus the major areas under which each person operates. Name index immediately follows this section. Section two, "Federal Officials with Liason Responsibility for Programs of Special Interest to Mexican Americans," includes agencies which administer programs "to assist in furthering the social and economic progress of the American people," and has a section which lists people specifically working with Mexican Americans. Section three, "National Private Organizations with Civil Rights Programs," is a cross-section of groups which are concerned almost exclusively with civil rights or those which have developed strong civil rights programs. Arranged alphabetically with address, telephone number, executive officers, purpose, size and publications listed for each. Section four lists official state agencies with civil rights responsibilities, by state. Planned to be an annual publication.

POLITICAL SCIENCE & INTERNATIONAL RELATIONS

GENERAL WORKS
BIBLIOGRAPHIES

100. U.S. Department of State. Bureau of Intelligence and Research. Office of Strategic and Functional Research. **Status of the World's Nations.** 4th ed. Washington, GPO, 1969. 20 p. $0.30. LC Card No. 64-61180. S 1.119/2:2/5

"Identifies 136 states generally accepted as independent and provides the geographic nomenclature officially recognized by the U.S. Government." Includes independent states, quasi-independent states and irregular categories of political areas and regimes. Gives both common and formal names for independent states. Appendix I lists populations, areas and capitals for independent states. Appendix II is a chronology of newly independent states since 1943.

101. U.S. Department of State. Foreign Service Institute. **This Changing World: A Reading Guide for the General Sessions.** Washington, Department of State, 1969. 58 p. Issuing Agency. S 1.114/3:W89

"This Reading Guide provides bibliographic support for the General Sessions program conducted by the Center for Area and Country Studies . . . a major concern [of which] is with continuity and change as they relate to development and modernization." The bibliography seeks to allow the problems of the changing world to be considered interrelatedly. Entries are under broad subject headings and are not annotated. No index.

DIRECTORIES

102. U.S. Department of State. **Foreign Affairs Research: A Directory of Governmental Resources.** Washington, GPO, 1969. 50 p. $0.55. LC Card No. 79-604442. S 1.2:F76a/4/969

Provides a broad descriptive listing of the many government resources accessible to the scholar who is engaged in social and behavioral science research on foreign areas and international affairs.

103. U.S. Department of State. **Foreign Consular Offices in the United States, 1969.** Rev. April 1969. Washington, GPO, 1969. 94 p. $0.35. LC Card No. 32-26478. S 1.69:128/5

A complete and official listing of the foreign consular offices in the United States together with their jurisdictions, recognized personnel and date of recognition.

104. U.S. Department of State. **List of Foreign Service Posts.** Washington, Department of State, 1968. 4 p. Issuing Agency. S 1.7:nos.

Supplement to **Foreign Service of the United States of America** and **Educational Preparation for Foreign Service Officers and Entrance Examinations.** Lists employment opportunities in foreign countries and cities where U.S. embassies or consultates are located.

DISARMAMENT

105. U.S. Arms Control and Disarmament Agency. **Documents on Disarmament, 1968, with Bibliography.** Comp. and annotated by Robert W. Lambert. Washington, GPO, 1969. 893 p. $3.75. LC Card No. 60-64408. AC 1.11/2: 968

Contains documents on the "nonproliferation treaty and other aspects of disarmament and arms control," arranged chronologically. Includes lists of principal organizations and conferences and of people involved in the field, and a bibliography. Complete subject index.

106. U.S. Library of Congress. **Arms Control and Disarmament: A Quarterly Bibliography with Abstracts and Annotations.** Washington, GPO, 1965– . Quarterly. $2.50/yr. LC Card No. 65-47970. LC 2.10:v.5, 1969

This bibliography "attempts to bring under . . . control a large and growing body of literature," and contains abstracts and annotations of current literature in English, French, German and Russian and other languages when an English translation exists. Arranged by subjects with author and subject indexes for each issue. The fourth issue each year contains cumulative author and subject indexes.

PEACE CORPS

107. U.S. Peace Corps. **Peace Corps Fact Book.** Washington, Peace Corps, 1969. 24 p. Issuing Agency. S 19.16:969

A "job-by-job description of Peace Corps programs which can be expected to enter training through the summer of 1970." Although intended primarily for prospective applicants, this is a very informative directory for anyone wanting information about the work of the Peace Corps. Arranged first by the geographic regions assigned by the Peace Corps for administrative purposes (i.e. Africa, Latin America, North Africa/Near East/South Asia, and East Asia and Pacific) as well as worldwide programs. Preceding the section on each region is a map of the area and a brief general description of it. The map itself names the countries and then has numbers which explain what areas of fields of work are being done in each one. The text is first by area of work, then alphabetical by country, then by program number listing the requirements for volunteers and the type of work they will do. A country may be listed more than once if, for example, it has a program in Sports/Recreation and one in Community Development. The index lists, by skill and academic area, the specialties required for the various programs and refers to the program numbers. The 1967 edition was titled: **Peace Corps Program Directory.**

RESEARCH

108. U.S. Department of State. Office of External Research. Bureau of Intelligence and Research. **University Centers of Foreign Affairs Research:**

A Directory. Washington, GPO, 1968. 139 p. $1.00. LC Card No. 68-60080.
S 1.2:Un3

One in a number of State Department directories of centers engaged in
international studies. This directory is focused on "U.S. university-affiliated
centers which have as their main purpose social science research in foreign
affairs," and "includes only those university research programs and projects
which are organized in easily identified centers or institutes." Arranged alphabetically by name of the university and gives a complete description of each
program including names of principal researchers, focus or emphasis of the
program, recent representative publications and studies in progress. A chronology of the development of foreign affairs research centers forms an appendix.

TREATIES

109. U.S. Department of State. **Foreign Relations of the United States,
Diplomatic Papers.** Washington, GPO, 1969, 7 vols. S 1.1:969

This monumental series, issued since 1861, contains the official records
of U.S. foreign policy, including "all documents needed to give a comprehensive record of the major foreign policy decisions within the range of the Department of State's responsibilities, together with appropriate materials concerning
the facts which contributed to the formulation of the policies." Each volume
covers only certain countries within a given year. Documents are arranged
chronologically under each country. In 1968 one volume was published covering 1944 and four for 1945. In 1969, four volumes for 1945 were issued and
three for 1946.

110a. U.S. Department of State. **United States Treaties and Other International
Agreements: V. 19, Pt. 2, 1968.** Washington, GPO, 1969. p. 1227-2619.
$12.75. LC Card No. 53-60242. S 9.12:19/pt.2

110b. U.S. Department of State. **United States Treaties and Other International
Agreements: V. 19, Pt. 3, 1968.** Washington, GPO, 1969. p. 2620-4087.
$13.25. LC Card No. 53-60242. S 9.12:19/pt.3

To be published in six parts. Lists multilateral treaties and general agreements on tariffs and trade reached at Geneva, June 30, 1967.

111. U.S. Department of State. **Treaties in Force.** Washington, GPO, 1969.
376 p. $1.50. LC Card No. 56-61604. S 9.14:969

Lists all treaties as well as other international agreements in force on
January 1, 1969 between the United States and foreign countries which have
been made by the President. Part one lists bilateral treaties and other agreements first by country and then by subjects. Part two lists multilateral treaties
and agreements by subject with names of participating countries after each
entry. Kept up-to-date during each year by the weekly issues of the Department of State **Bulletin.**

NATIONAL GOVERNMENTS

DIRECTORIES

112. U.S. Department of State. **Chiefs of State and Cabinet Members of Foreign Governments.** Washington, Department of State, 1969. 70 p. Issuing Agency. S 1.113/2:69-22

"Includes as many governments of the world as is considered practicable, some of them not yet fully independent and others not officially recognized by the United States." Arranged alphabetically by country with names and titles of officials listed. Revised frequently.

113. U.S. Department of State. Bureau of Intelligence and Research. Office of Strategic and Functional Research. **Africa: Pattern of Sovereignty.** Washington, GPO, 1968. 17 p. $0.20. LC Card No. 68-62588. S 1.119/2:6/2

"Designed to summarize in convenient fashion some of the information relevant to the understanding of the countless adjustments which are taking place" in Africa. Describes the background of the new states; explains the political-geographic factors which account for their existence; discusses the complex boundary changes. Tables show new African states, 1950-68, capitals, areas, populations and nationality forms for major countries, and those areas of Africa which were realms of European countries as of 1950.

114. U.S. Department of State. Bureau of Intelligence and Research. Office of Strategic and Functional Research. **Commonwealth of Nations.** Washington, GPO, 1968. 44 p. $0.35. S 1.119/2:8

"Eighth in a series of national sovereignties and related geographic data." Gives brief sketches on the locations, historic highlights, political developments, forms of government, and administrative structures of all countries of the Commonwealth and the dependencies. "Material contained in this study will be of use to all agencies concerned with international affairs, and will also be beneficial to libraries, schools and commercial establishments."

UNITED STATES

GENERAL WORKS

115. U.S. Bureau of the Census. **Congressional District Atlas.** Washington, GPO, 1968. 203 p. $1.75. LC Card No. A66-7901. C 3.62/5:968

Official maps for congressional representatives. Counties of the United States are keyed to maps of their Congressional Districts. Shows all redistricting as of August 1968.

116. U.S. House of Representatives. Committee on Post Office and Civil Service. **United States Government Policy and Supporting Positions.** Washington, GPO, 1968. 162 p. $2.00. Y 4.P84/10:P75

This publication is a result of a request from the Committee on Post Office and Civil Service that the Civil Service Commission conduct a survey of excepted positions in the federal civil service. The excepted positions include presidential appointments, noncareer executive assignment positions in GS 16-18, other excepted positions at GS 12 and above, and positions under specified Schedule A and B authorities. Includes personnel in all branches of the government, by office or agency with the person's location, position, name, type of appointment, grade or salary, tenure and date of expiration of the appointment.

All information is as of September 30, 1968 and therefore does not reflect changes in personnel which occurred with the Nixon administration.

DIRECTORIES

117. U.S. Bureau of the Census. **Finances of Municipalities and Township Governments.** Washington, GPO, 1969. 255 p. $2.00. LC Card No. A68-7201. C 3.145/4:967/v.4/no.4

Covers four major subject fields: governmental organization, taxable property values, public employment and governmental finances for two of the five major classes of local government (i.e. municipalities and townships). Includes statistics on revenues, expenditures, utility finances, indebtedness, cash and security holdings and other aspects of finance in both township governments and municipalities. Includes a glossary of selected terms.

118. U.S. Senate. **Election Law Guidebook, 1968, Summary of Federal and State Laws Regulating Nomination and Election of United States Senators.** Prep. by Elizabeth Yadlosky and Robert L. Tienken. Rev. ed. Washington, GPO, 1968. 180 p. $0.50. LC Card No. 52-60536. Ser. 12798-1 Sen. Doc. 90th Congress No. 76

"Designed for ready reference, giving in tabular or short summary form the highlights of the provisions of Federal and State laws pertaining to the election of senators." Includes reference to the actual laws, a list of when primary elections are held in various states, rules regarding nominating papers or petitions, rules regarding campaign expenditures, election offenses and states where applicable, and a list of states which have write-in provisions.

OFFICIAL REGISTERS

119. U.S. Congress. Joint Committee on Printing. **Congressional Pictorial Directory, Ninety-First Congress, January 1969.** Washington, GPO, 1969. 202 p. Illus. $2.75. LC Card No. 68-61223. Y 4.P93/1:1p/91

An illustrated pocket directory of members of Congress. Includes photographs of Congressmen, a list of state delegations and an alphabetical list by name of senators and representatives.

120. U.S. Congress. Joint Committee on Printing. **Official Congressional Directory—91st Congress, 1st Session (beginning January 3, 1969).** Washington, GPO, 1969. 1025 p. $4.00 (regular edition); $5.50 (thumb indexed edition). LC Card No. 6-35330. Y 4.P93/1:1/91-1

Includes biographies by state of senators and representatives; delegations by state with names of senators and representatives; alphabetical lists of senate and house memberships with home address, Washington address, and page number of biographies; chronological lists of terms in office by year of expiration, by years of continuous service, congresses in which they have served; lists of committees and members; administrative assistants and secretaries; statistical information on sessions of Congress, votes cast in last elections for senators, representatives and governors; officers of the Senate and House; officers in executive departments and independent agencies; biographies of members of the Supreme Court; government of the District of Columbia; list of international organizations and officials; foreign diplomatic and consular offices; members of the press admitted to House and Senate galleries, newspapers represented, photographers admitted, television and radio newsmen admitted; and maps of congressional districts. Altogether, there is biographical material on 1500 top staff personnel in the legislative branch, all cross-indexed. Includes a general index of names. Supplemented by the **Congressional Pictorial Directory** (q.v.), which includes photographs of congressmen.

121. U.S. National Archives and Records Service. Office of the Federal Register. **U.S. Government Organization Manual, 1969-70.** Washington, GPO, 1969. 805 p. $3.00. LC Card No. 35-26025. GS 4.109:969

Known simply as the "Organization Manual," this is an invaluable reference aid for any library or person. It is the official organization handbook of the federal government. Contains sections which describe the agencies of the legislative, judicial, and executive branches as well as descriptions of the independent agencies and selected international organizations. Includes lists of current officials, organization charts for the more complex departments, appendixes on abolished or transferred agencies and functions, government publications and an alphabetical list of assignments in the Code of Federal Regulations. Also includes a complete name index and a subject/departmental index.

122. U.S. Department of State. **The Biographic Register, July 1969.** Washington, GPO, 1969. 464 p. (State Department and Foreign Service Series 126, Publication 7722). $4.50. LC Card No. 9-22072. S 1.69:126/4

"The **Biographic Register** provides information and background on personnel of the Department of State and the Foreign Service, and other Federal Government Agencies that participate in the field of foreign affairs." Biographies are arranged alphabetically by name of ambassadors, ministers, chiefs of missions, Foreign Services officers, etc., classes 1 through 4 and Civil Service employees GS 12 and above.

U.S. PRESIDENTS

123. U.S. Library of Congress. **Index to the James K. Polk Papers.** Washington, GPO, 1969. 91 p. (Presidents' Papers Index Series). $1.25. LC Card No. 73-600928. LC 4.7:P75

The **Index** was prepared to accompany the microfilm copies of the Polk Papers made available in 1969 from the Photoduplication Service of the Library of Congress. Contents of the **Index** include provenance, description of papers, reel list, how to use the index and the computer produced index to names. Indexes papers available in the Library of Congress reproduced on 67 reels of microfilm.

124. U.S. Library of Congress. **Presidential Inaugurations, A Selected List of References.** Washington, GPO, 1969. 230 p. $2.00. LC 2.2:P92/3/969

This bibliography presents a selected list of references compiled to serve as a guide to useful information on inaugural ceremonies and festivities from 1789 tò the present.

125. U.S. National Archives and Records Service. Franklin D. Roosevelt Library. **Era of Franklin Delano Roosevelt: a Selected Bibliography of Periodical and Dissertation Literature, 1945-66.** Comp. and annotated by William J. Stewart. Washington, National Archives and Records Service (1967) 1969. 175 p. $2.50 (from the Franklin D. Roosevelt Library, Hyde Park, N.Y. 12538). LC Card No. 70-602361. GS 4.17/3:R67/945-66

This bibliography excludes those publications which are concerned purely with military operations, newspaper articles, and unsigned articles. It is divided into four sections: (1) Franklin D. Roosevelt; (2) New Deal; (3) World War II; (4) Archives, Bibliography and Historiography. Annotations give the scope and nature of the work without evaluative or critical comment. Indexed by authors and subjects with a list of serials cited.

ARMED FORCES

126. U.S. Department of Defense. Joint Chiefs of Staff. **Dictionary of United States Military Terms for Joint Usage.** Rev. ed. Washington, GPO, 1968. 322 p. $2.00. LC Card No. 59-62410. D 5.12:1/968

Short Title: **JD**

"Prepared under the direction of the Joint Chiefs of Staff in coordination with the military services for planning and operational usage" with the purpose of standardization of military terms and definitions. Incorporates NATO, SEATO, and CENTO glossaries. Appendices contain terms and definitions which are part of a comprehensive worldwide program of standardization in certain functional areas. Terms designated with "JCS" before the definition are not defined elsewhere in the Department of Defense.

127. U.S. Department of the Navy. Naval Operations Office. **Dictionary of American Naval Fighting Ships.** Washington, GPO, 1959— . 4v (to date). LC Card No. 60-60198. D 207.10:nos.1-

Published to date: Vol. 1 (1959)— A-B ($3.00)
Vol. 2 (1963)— C-F (o.p.)
Vol. 3 (1968)— G-K ($6.00)
Vol. 4 (1969)— L-M ($7.50)

When completed, this work will make available basic information on every naval ship that has "served its part in shaping the history . . . of the United States." Its purpose is to "give the concise facts about every ship so that it may be a ready reference for those who have served in the ships and for the student, writer, and many others who seek a work like this." The descriptions of each ship include tonnage, length, beam, draft, speed, armament, and class; and where known, the builder, sponsor, launching and commission dates, date of acquisition by the Navy, first commanding officer, and a concise operational history. Each volume also includes a bibliography, appendixes for various types of ships in the modern and historic Navy, and illustrations. Expected to be completed by 1976.

128. U.S. National Museum. **United States Army Headgear to 1854: Catalog of United States Army Uniforms in the Collections of the Smithsonian Institution, volume 1.** By Edgar M. Howell and Donald E. Kloster. Washington, GPO, 1969. 75 p. Illus. $2.75. LC Card No. 73-601. SI 3.3:269

This is the first in a projected series on army dress based on collections of the Museum of History and Technology of the Smithsonian Institution. "Specifically it is a descriptive, critical and documentary catalog of the Regular Establishment through 1854." Other volumes will cover headgear from 1854 to the present, uniforms, and footwear. Pictures of the headgear are provided, as are detailed narrative descriptions, regulations for wear and source notes for each item. The appendix lists makers of headgear and dates. A bibliography is also provided.

129. U.S. Naval Operations Office. **Naval Documents of the American Revolution, vol. 4.** Ed. by William Bell Clark. Washington, GPO, 1969. 1580 p. $14.25. LC Card No. 64-60087. D 207.12:4

Documents are arranged chronologically under three main divisions: the American Theatre, February 19-April 17, 1776; the European Theatre, February 1-May 25, 1776, and the American Theatre, April 18-May 8, 1776. Three appendixes and a bibliography supplement the documents. Includes a very detailed subject index.

130. U.S. Department of the Navy. Naval History Division. **United States Naval History, A Bibliography.** 5th ed. Washington, GPO, 1969. 34 p. Illus. $0.35. LC Card No. 71-604014. D 207.11:H62/969

This selective list includes materials useful for large schools, public and college libraries. Arranged under broad categories such as Bibliography, General Histories, Biographies, Naval history by periods, Marine Corps history, Coast Guard history and special subjects. Author index; no annotations.

For more comprehensive coverage see **U.S. Naval History Sources in the Washington Area and Suggested Research Subjects** (Washington, GPO, 1965 rev.).

131. U.S. Military Academy. **Bibliography of Military History; a Selected,**

Annotated Listing of Reference Sources in the United States Military Academy Library. Comp. by J. Thomas Russell. West Point, N.Y., U.S. Military Academy, 1969. 57 p. Issuing Agency. D 109.10:7

Lists works chosen for their "practical, informational value as sources for the beginning researcher in the field of military history." Arranged by broad subjects patterned after the arrangement in Winchell's **Guide to Reference Books** (8th edition). Annotations are adapted from Winchell. Not indexed.

GEOGRAPHY

GENERAL WORKS

132. U.S. Department of State. Bureau of Intelligence and Research. Office of Strategic and Functional Research. **Sovereignty of the Sea.** Rev. ed. Washington, GPO, 1969. 33 p. $0.40. LC Card No. 65-61761. S 1.119/2:3/2

"This Bulletin . . . concerns the rights which the United States and other countries have on, over, and under the surface of the sea." Includes material for background and reference but not for legal decisions. Two main sections contain information on the geography of the ocean environment and background on offshore lines of jurisdiction which delineate sovereignty and rights. Appendixes contain related material (e.g. a selected bibliography, a list of charts to be used in identifying offshore features). Includes tables of coastline and ocean measurements.

ATLASES AND MAPS

133. U.S. Library of Congress. **Detroit and Vicinity before 1900; An Annotated List of Maps.** Comp. by Alberta G. Auringer Koerner. Washington, GPO, 1968. 84 p. $0.45. LC Card No. 68-67060. LC 5.2:D48

Compiled to "facilitate cartographic research concerned with this historic area of the Great Lakes region," this bibliography describes 239 maps and atlases which depict the city of Detroit, Michigan, its vicinity, the Detroit River, Wayne County and other towns in Wayne County during the 18th and 19th centuries. Also includes atlases and maps depicting the adjacent shore in Canada regardless of publication date. Arranged first chronologically by date on the map, then alphabetically by author or title. Provides full information (i.e. author, title, imprint and scale) for each entry. Indexes significant titles, authors, cartographers, surveyors, lithographers, publishers, counties, and cities and towns (other than Detroit).

134. U.S. Library of Congress. **Facsimiles of Rare Historical Maps; A List of Reproductions for Sale by Various Publishers and Distributors.** Comp. by Walter W. Ristow. 3d ed., rev. and enl. Washington, Library of Congress, 1968. 20 p. Issuing Agency. LC Card No. 66-62298. LC 5.2:H62/3:968

This list includes facsimiles distributed by nonprofit institutions and by commercial publishers and dealers. Maps and atlases are listed under the name of the publisher or distributor with size or number of pages, cost and description. Indexed by personal and place names.

PUBLIC LANDS

135a. U.S. Department of the Interior. Library. **Public Lands Bibliography, Supplement II.** Comp. by the Reference Section. Springfield, Va., Clearinghouse, 1968. 37 p. Issuing Agency. I 22.9/2:7

Arranged alphabetically by author under three headings: (1) Articles and monographs; (2) Laws and legislation; (3) Theses. NUC code designations are provided to indicate the libraries where each publication can be found. Includes materials published from 1965 through October 1967. Arranged with articles, monographs, and theses in one section, and laws enacted during 1964-67, hearings, House and Senate Reports, and committee prints in a second section.

135b. U.S. Federal Committee on Research Natural Areas. **A Directory of Research Natural Areas on Federal Lands of the United States of America.** Washington, GPO, 1968. 129 p. $0.70. LC Card No. 68-61218. Y 3.F31/ 19:9/968

Describes "more than 300 natural areas set aside on Federal lands for scientific and educational purposes." Published for three purposes: (1) it is an inventory of the research natural areas already established; (2) it is a means of determining what additional areas are needed; and (3) it is an announcement of the "availability of these natural areas for appropriate use of scientists and educators." Arranged by primary type of area and then alphabetically by name. Includes a list of areas by state. Indexes to common names and scientific names.

HISTORY & AREA STUDIES

ARCHAEOLOGY

136. U.S. Smithsonian Institution. **Bibliography of Salvage Archeology in the United States.** Comp. by Jerome E. Petsche. Washington, Smithsonian Institution, 1968. 162 p. Issuing Agency. LC Card No. 68-67086. SI 1.22:10

Published with the assistance of a grant from the American Council of Learned Societies to the Committee for the Recovery of Archeological Remains.

"This bibliography is primarily a guide to appraisals and reports of archeological and paleontological remains lost or threatened as a result of the numerous projects for irrigation, flood control, hydroelectric power, and navigation improvement in the river basins of the United States." Arranged by state with articles and books about that state alphabetically by author. Not annotated. Appendixes contain cross references to articles containing substantial information other than or in addition to archeology.

AFRICA

137. U.S. Department of State. Foreign Service Institute. Center for Area and Country Studies. **Near East and North Africa, Selected Functional and Country Bibliography.** Washington, Department of State, 1968. 43 p. Issuing Agency. LC Card No. 68-60921. S 1.114/3:N27

Lists publications in the English language relevant to the Near East and North Africa. Arranged alphabetically by author under 25 subject headings. Not annotated or indexed. Mimeographed.

138. U.S. Department of the Air Force. Air University Library. **Africa, Selected References.** Maxwell Air Force Base, Ala., Air University, 1968. 86 p. Issuing Agency. D 301.26/11:159, supp. 8, pt. 1

An alphabetical listing of references to books and periodical articles on Africa and on individual regions and countries in Africa, arranged under the following subjects: economics, communist penetration, conferences, politics, military aspects, psycho-social factors. Not annotated or indexed.

Part 2 of this bibliography is classified and can only be used by persons with the proper security clearance.

BURUNDI

139. U.S. Department of the Army. **Area Handbook for Burundi.** By Gordon G. McDonald and others. Prep. by Foreign Area Studies, American University. Washington, GPO, 1969. 203 p. Illus. $2.75. LC Card No. 70-605915. D 101.22:550-83

One of a series of handbooks designed for military and other personnel who need a convenient compilation of basic facts on specific countries. Provides a comprehensive survey of the society of Burundi. A brief, quick reference summary in the front gives basic facts on the country, government, population, climate, etc. and cites recent legislation in regard to citizenship and other vital areas. Arranged in four major sections: Social, Political, Economic and National Security, with numerous chapter divisions on specific topics. Additional materials include a bibliography, a glossary and an index.

GHANA

140. U.S. Library of Congress. Reference Department. **Ghana: A Guide to the Official Publications, 1872-1968.** Comp. by Julian W. Witherell and Sharon B. Lockwood. Washington, GPO, 1969. 110 p. $1.25. LC Card No. 74-601680. LC 2.8:G34/872-968

"This guide to official publications of Ghana lists the published government records from 1872 . . . to 1968. It includes publications of the Gold Coast (1872-1957) and Ghana (1957-68) and a selection of British Government documents relating specifically to the Gold Coast, Ghana and British Togoland." Index to personal authors and subjects.

GUYANA

141. U.S. Department of the Army. **Area Handbook for Guyana.** By William B. Mitchell and others. Prep. by Foreign Area Studies, American University. Washington, GPO, 1969. 378 p. Illus. $3.25. LC Card No. 79-606159. D 101.22:550-82

One of a series of handbooks designed for military and other personnel who need a convenient compilation of basic facts on specific countries. Provides a comprehensive survey of the society of Guyana. A brief, quick reference summary in the front gives basic facts on the country, government, population, climate, etc. and cites recent legislation in regard to citizenship and other vital areas. Arranged in four major sections: Social, Political, Economic and National Security, with numerous chapter divisions on specific topics. Additional materials include a bibliography, a glossary and an index.

LIBYA

142. U.S. Department of the Army. **Area Handbook for Libya.** By Stanford Research Institute. Washington, GPO, 1969. 307 p. Illus. $3.00. LC Card No. 77-606555. D 101.22:550-85

One of a series of handbooks designed for military and other personnel who need a convenient compilation of basic facts on specific countries. Provides a comprehensive survey of the society of Libya. A brief, quick reference summary in the front gives basic facts on the country, government, population, climate, etc. and cites recent legislation in regard to citizenship and other vital areas. Arranged in four major sections: Social, Political, Economic and National Security, with numerous chapter divisions on specific topics. Additional materials include a bibliography, a glossary and an index.

MOZAMBIQUE

143. U.S. Department of the Army. **Area Handbook for Mozambique.** By Allison Butler Herrick and others. Prep. by Foreign Area Studies, American

University. Washington, GPO, 1969. 351 p. Illus. $3.25. D 101.22:550-64

One of a series of handbooks prepared for military and other personnel by Foreign Area Studies of the American University, Washington. It provides a comprehensive survey of the society of Mozambique as of the first part of 1967: Research and writing was completed July, 1967 but this was not published until 1969. A brief quick reference summary in the front of the book provides basic facts on the country, government, population, climate, etc. and cites recent legislation in regard to citizenship and other vital areas. Arranged in four major sections: Social, Political, Economic and National Security, with numerous chapter divisions on specific topics. Additional materials include a bibliography, a glossary and an index.

RWANDA

144. U.S. Department of the Army. **Area Handbook for Rwanda.** By Richard F. Nyrop and others. Prep. by Foreign Area Studies, American University. Washington, GPO, 1969. 212 p. Illus. $2.75. LC Card No. 72-606089. D 101.22:550-84

One of a series of handbooks designed for military and other personnel who need a convenient compilation of basic facts on specific countries. Provides a comprehensive survey of the society of Rwanda. A brief, quick reference summary in the front gives basic facts on the country, government, population, climate, etc., and cites recent legislation in regard to citizenship and other vital areas. Arranged in four major sections: Social, Political, Economic and National Security, with numerous chapter divisions on specific topics. Additional materials include a bibliography, a glossary and an index.

TANZANIA

145. U.S. Department of the Army. **Area Handbook for Tanzania.** By Allison Butler Herrick and others. Prep. by Foreign Area Studies, American University. Washington, GPO, 1968. 522 p. Illus. $3.75. LC Card No. 68-67374. D 101.22:550-62

One of a series of handbooks designed for military and other personnel who need a convenient compilation of basic facts on specific countries. Provides a comprehensive survey of the society of Tanzania. A brief, quick reference summary in the front gives basic facts on the country, government, population, climate, etc. and cites recent legislation in regard to citizenship and other vital areas. Arranged in four major sections: Social, Political, Economic and National Security, with numerous chapter divisions on specific topics. Additional materials include a bibliography, a glossary and an index.

UGANDA

146. U.S. Department of the Army. **Area Handbook for Uganda.** By Allison Butler Herrick. Prep. by Foreign Area Studies, American University. Washington, GPO, 1969. 456 p. Illus. $3.50. LC Card No. 73-601330. D 101.22:550-74

One of a series of handbooks designed for military and other personnel who need a convenient compilation of basic facts on specific countries. Provides a comprehensive survey of the society of Uganda. A brief, quick reference summary in the front gives basic facts on the country, government, population, climate, etc. and cites recent legislation in regard to citizenship and other vital areas. Arranged in four major sections: Social, Political, Economic and National Security, with numerous chapter divisions on specific topics. Additional materials include a bibliography, a glossary and an index.

ZAMBIA

147. U.S. Department of the Army. **Area Handbook for Zambia.** By Irving Kaplan and others. Prep. by Foreign Area Studies, American University. Washington, GPO, 1969. 482 p. Illus. $3.75. LC Card No. 79-604730. D 101.22:550-75

One of a series of handbooks designed for military and other personnel who need a convenient compilation of basic facts on specific countries. Provides a comprehensive survey of the society of Zambia. A brief, quick reference summary in the front gives basic facts on the country, government, population, climate, etc. and cites recent legislation in regard to citizenship and other vital areas. Arranged in four major sections: Social, Political, Economic and National Security, with numerous chapter divisions on specific topics. Additional materials include a bibliography, a glossary and an index.

THE AMERICAS

LATIN AMERICA

148. U.S. Department of State. Foreign Service Institute. Center for Area and Country Studies. **Latin America, Selected Functional and Country Bibliography.** Washington, Department of State, 1968. 2 v. Issuing Agency. LC Card No. 68-67047. S 1.114/3:L34/pt.1 & 2
    Pt. 1—Latin American Area
    Pt. 2—Countries of Latin America

Lists publications, in the English language, about Latin America. Arranged alphabetically by author under 25 major subject headings in each volume. Not annotated or indexed. Mimeographed.

149. U.S. Department of the Air Force. Air University Library. **Latin America, Selected References.** Maxwell Air Force Base, Ala., Air University, 1968. 26 p. Issuing Agency. D 301.26/11:166(rev.), supp.3, pt. 1

An alphabetical listing of references to books and periodical articles on Latin America arranged under the following headings: economics, communist penetration, conferences and alliances, education, politics and government, military aspects, and psycho-social aspects. Not annotated or indexed.

Part 2 of this bibliography is classified and can only be used by persons with the proper security clearance.

150. U.S. Department of the Army. **Latin America and the Caribbean; an Analytic Survey of the Literature.** Washington, GPO, 1969. 319 p. Illus. $8.25. LC Card No. 76-603569. D 101.22:550-7

"This survey of recent literature offers a convenient reference source, particularly in matters of defense and national security." The 900 citations are arranged under broad topics such as "Latin American: An Economic Asset" and subdivided by more specific subject areas. Each entry is fully annotated. Includes a section of source materials for research and reference. The appendix contains reprints of the Department of State's **Background Notes** on the various countries of Latin America. Many maps are also included.

ARGENTINA

151. U.S. Department of the Army. **Area Handbook for Argentina.** By Frederick P. Munson and others. Prep. by Foreign Area Studies, American University. Washington, GPO, 1969. 446 p. Illus. $3.50. LC Card No. 78-605289. D 101.22:550-73

One of a series of handbooks designed for military and other personnel who need a convenient compilation of basic facts on specific countries. Provides a comprehensive survey of the society of Argentina. A brief, quick reference summary in the front gives basic facts on the country, government, population, climate, etc. and cites recent legislation in regard to citizenship and other vital areas. Arranged in four major sections: Social, Political, Economic and National Security, with numerous chapter divisions on specific topics. Additional materials include a bibliography, a glossary and an index.

UNITED STATES

152. U.S. National Historical Publications Commission. **Writings on American History, 1959: Annual Report of the American Historical Associations, 1961, v. 2.** Ed. by James R. Masterson. Washington, GPO, 1969. 737 p. $4.75. LC Card No. 4-18261. SI 4.1:961/v.2

This volume, a classified list of 9,114 books and articles on United States history that were published during 1959, continues a series begun with the issuance of a volume that listed writings published in 1902. Including the present volume, the series consists of 47 volumes covering 49 years. Volumes for 1904-5 and 1941-47 have not been prepared. Since 1951 the Commission has assumed responsibility for preparation of the **Writings,** but it is published as a part of the American Historical Association's Annual Report. Contains three parts: the historical profession, the United States, and regions of the United States. Parts I and II are subdivided by topic and part III is divided geographically. The list excludes newspapers, historical fiction, juvenile works, archaeological reports, genealogical works, and writings concerned with very recent events. Includes a list of serials cited and an index.

153. U.S. National Park Service. **Explorers and Settlers, Historic Places Commemorating Early Exploration and Settlement of the United States.** Robert G. Ferris, ed. Washington, GPO, 1968. 506 p. $3.50. LC Card No. 66-60013. I 29.2:H62/9/v.5

Series Title: National Survey of Historic Sites and Buildings, v. 5.

The purpose of this volume is to "focus attention on, and stimulate further activities in, the field of historic preservation." Part one is a brief narrative background for the period of early exploration and settlement. The second part consists of "evaluations and descriptions of the historic sites and structures" of the period. Includes end-notes, a list of selected readings and a comprehensive index.

CIVIL WAR

154. U.S. Marine Corps. **Annotated Bibliography of the United States Marines in the Civil War.** By Michael O'Quinlivan and Rowland P. Gill. Rev. ed. Washington, Marine Corps, 1968. 15 p. Issuing Agency. LC Card No. 68-62467. D 214.15:C49

"Published for the information of all who are interested in the history of the Marine Corps during the Civil War." Bibliography consists of materials dealing specifically with Marines of both sides in the Civil War, although a few general works are also included. Lists books and journal articles. Annotated. No index.

MANUSCRIPTS & ARCHIVES

155. U.S. Military Academy. **Preliminary Guide to the Manuscript Collection of the U.S. Military Academy Library.** Comp. by J. Thomas Russell. West Point, N.Y., U.S. Military Academy, 1968. 260 p. Issuing Agency. D 109.10:5

Issued as an aid to researchers, collectors and librarians, this guide contains citations to the manuscript holdings in the library of the U.S. Military Academy before October 1967, including both analyzed and unanalyzed collections. Describes collections in terms of physical space, type of documents, how acquired, and names of people or subjects prominent in the collection.

156. U.S. National Archives and Records Service. **Guide to the Archives of Government of the Confederate States of America.** By Henry Putney Beers. Washington, GPO, 1968. 536 p. $3.75. LC Card No. A68-7603. GS 4.6/1: C76

A descriptive guide to the extant records of both the United States Government and the government of the Confederate States of America. A companion to the **Guide to Federal Archives Relating to the Civil War** (1962). Lists records of the Confederate States followed by those of Congress, the Judiciary, the Presidency, the Departments of State, the Treasury, War, Navy, Post Office and Justice.

157. U.S. National Archives and Records Service. **List of Record Groups in the National Archives and the Federal Records Centers.** Washington, General Services Administration, 1969. 39 p. Issuing Agency. GS 4.19:969

Lists record groups, in the first section, alphabetically by key work together with the record group number and a symbol for the unit having archival control over the group. The second part lists groups under operating units with control over them. Part three is by record group number.

REVOLUTIONARY WAR

158. U.S. Library of Congress. **American Revolution; Selected Reading List.** Washington, GPO, 1968. 39 p. $0.50. LC Card No. 68-67236. LC 1.12/2:R32

This bibliography cites books dealing with the period from the beginning of the controversy with Great Britain to the postwar years of the 1780's, and was published as a contribution to the Bicentennial of the American Revolution. Citations are listed under broad subjects with separate sections for biographies, personal narratives and documentary sources, children's literature and fiction. Author index.

ANTARCTICA

159. U.S. Library of Congress. **Antarctic Bibliography, v. 3, 1968.** Geza T. Thuranyi, ed. Prep. by the Library of Congress and sponsored by the Office of Antarctic Programs, National Science Foundation. Washington, GPO, 1968. 491 p. $6.00. LC Card No. 65-61825. LC 33.9:3

This volume is the third in a continuing series of compilations presenting abstracts and indexes of current (since 1962) Antarctic literature. Cut off date for this volume is February 1968; represents publications issued in 17 languages from 1962-68, with nearly 80% published between 1965 and 1967. Abstracts are published in groups of 2000 with cumulative indexes: volume 1 (1965) contains items 1-2000; volume 2 (1966) items 2001-4000; and this volume items 4001-6000. Material is arranged under 13 broad subject categories. Abstracts are by accession numbers and classified by Universal Decimal Classification System. Foreign language titles are given in English translation with the original title following in brackets using Library of Congress transliteration for Cyrillic and romanization of oriental languages. Indexed by author, subject and geographical area.

ASIA & MIDDLE EAST

GENERAL WORKS

160a. U.S. Department of the Air Force. Air University Library. **South Asia, Selected References.** Comp. by Florine Oltman. Maxwell Air Force Base, Ala., Air University, 1968. 24 p. Issuing agency. D 301.26/11:192

An alphabetical listing of references to books and periodical articles on South Asia arranged under the following headings: economic aspects, foreign relations, South Asia and the United States, military aspects, political aspects, psycho-social aspects and communism.

160b. U.S. Department of the Air Force. Air University Library. **South Asia, Selected Unclassified References.** Comp. by Florine Oltman. Maxwell Air Force Base, Ala., Air University, 1969. 14 p. Issuing Agency. D 301.26/11: 192, supp.1, pt.1

Part 2 of this supplement is classified and can only be used by persons with the proper security clearance.

AFGHANISTAN

161. U.S. Department of the Army. **Area Handbook for Afghanistan.** By Harvey H. Smith. Prep. by Foreign Area Studies, American University. Washington, GPO, 1969. 435 p. Illus. $3.50. LC Card No. 79-601329. D 101.22: 550-65

One of a series of handbooks designed for military and other personnel who need a convenient compilation of basic facts on specific countries. Provides a comprehensive survey of the society of Afghanistan. A brief, quick reference summary in the front gives basic facts on the country, government, population, climate, etc. and cites recent legislation in regard to citizenship and other vital areas. Arranged in four major sections: Social, Political, Economic and National Security, with numerous chapter divisions on specific topics. Additional materials include a bibliography, a glossary and an index.

CAMBODIA

162. U.S. Department of the Army. **Area Handbook for Cambodia.** By Frederick P. Munson and others. Prep. by Foreign Area Studies, American University. Washington, GPO, 1968. 364 p. Illus. $3.00. LC Card No. 72-600172. D 101.22:550-50

One of a series of handbooks designed for military and other personnel who need a convenient compilation of basic facts on specific countries. Provides a comprehensive survey of the society of Cambodia before the ouster of Prince Sihanouk. A brief, quick reference summary in the front gives basic facts on the country, government, population, climate, etc. and cites recent legislation in regard to citizenship and other vital areas. Arranged in four major sections: Social, Political, Economic and National Security, with numerous chapter divisions on specific topics. Additional materials include a bibliography, a glossary and an index.

INDIA

163. U.S. Library of Congress. **Accessions List: India, Annual Supplement: Cumulative List of Serials, 1969.** New Delhi, American Libraries Book Procurement Center: Washington, Library of Congress, 1969. 453 p. Issuing Agency. LC Card No. 63-24164. LC 1.30/1-2:969

Record of all Indian serials acquired by the U.S. Library of Congress American Libraries Procurement Center in New Delhi which were distributed to certain U.S. research libraries participating in Public Law 480 program. Arranged alphabetically by author. Supersedes previous monthly serial lists.

IRAQ

164. U.S. Department of the Army. **Area Handbook for Iraq.** By Harvey H. Smith and others. Prep. by Foreign Area Studies, American University.

Washington, GPO, 1969. 411 p. Illus. $3.50. LC Card No. 72-602177.
D 101.22:550-31

One of a series of handbooks designed for military and other personnel who need a convenient compilation of basic facts on individual countries. Provides a comprehensive survey of the society of Iraq. A brief, quick reference summary in the front provides basic facts on the country, government, population, climate, etc. and cites recent legislation in regard to citizenship and other vital areas. Arranged in four major sections: Social, Political, Economic and National Security, with numerous chapter divisions on specific topics. Additional materials include a bibliography, a glossary and an index.

JAPAN

165. U.S. Department of the Army. **Area Handbook for Japan.** By Frederic H. Chaffee and others. Prep. by Foreign Area Studies, American University. Washington, GPO, 1969. 628 p. Illus. $4.25. LC Card No. 73-605269.
D 101.22:550-30/2

One of a series of handbooks designed for military and other personnel who need a convenient compilation of basic facts on various countries. Provides a comprehensive survey of the society of Japan. A brief, quick reference summary in the front provides basic facts on the country, government, population, climate, etc. and cites recent legislation in regard to citizenship and other vital areas. Arranged in four major sections: Social, Political, Economic and National Security, with numerous chapter divisions on specific topics. Additional materials include a bibliography, a glossary and an index.

JORDAN

166. U.S. Department of the Army. **Area Handbook for the Hashemite Kingdom of Jordan.** By Howard C. Reese and others. Prep. for the American University by Systems Research Corp. under the auspices of Foreign Area Studies. Washington, GPO, 1969. 370 p. Illus. $3.25. LC Card No. 79-606088. D 101.22:550-34

One of a series of handbooks designed for military and other personnel who need a convenient compilation of basic facts on specific countries. Provides a comprehensive survey of the society of Jordan. A brief, quick reference summary in the front gives basic facts on the country, government, population, climate, etc. and cites recent legislation in regard to citizenship and other vital areas. Arranged in four major sections: Social, Political, Economic and National Security, with numerous chapter divisions on specific topics. Additional materials include a bibliography, a glossary and an index.

KOREA

167. U.S. Department of the Army. **Area Handbook for North Korea.** By Rinn-Sup Shinn and others. Prep. by Foreign Area Studies, American University. Washington, GPO, 1969. 481 p. Illus. $3.75. LC Card No. 75-605343.
D 101.22:550-81

One of a series of handbooks designed for military and other personnel who need a convenient compilation of basic facts on specific countries. Provides a comprehensive survey of the society of North Korea. A brief, quick reference summary in the front gives basic facts on the country, government, population, climate, etc. and cites recent legislation in regard to citizenship and other vital areas. Arranged in four major sections: Social, Political, Economic and National Security, with numerous chapter divisions on specific topics. Additional materials include a bibliography, a glossary and an index.

168. U.S. Department of the Army. **Area Handbook for the Republic of Korea.** By Kenneth G. Clare and others. Prepared for the American University by Westwood Research, Inc. Washington, GPO, 1969. 492 p. Illus. $3.75. LC Card No. 78-604178. D 101.22:550-41

One of a series of handbooks designed for military and other personnel who need a convenient compilation of basic facts on specific countries. Provides a comprehensive survey of the society of Korea. A brief, quick reference summary in the front gives basic facts on the country, government, population, climate, etc. and cites recent legislation in regard to citizenship and other vital areas. Arranged in four major sections: Social, Political, Economic and National Security, with numerous chapter divisions on specific topics. Additional materials include a bibliography, a glossary and an index.

LEBANON

169. U.S. Department of the Army. **Area Handbook for Lebanon.** By Harvey H. Smith and others. Prep. by Foreign Area Studies, American University. Rev. ed. Washington, GPO, 1969. 352 p. Illus. $3.25. LC Card No. 72-603935. D 101.22:550-24

A compact descriptive presentation of the social, political and economic aspects of Lebanon. Attempts to analyze and indicate the impact of the past decade of changes on the country's external and internal situations. Text is divided into four broad sections: social, political, economic and national security with numerous chapter subdivisions. Lists many illustrations and tables. Also includes a bibliography, a glossary and an index.

MIDDLE EAST

170. U.S. Armed Forces Information Service. **Pocket Guide to the Middle East.** Washington, GPO, 1969. 116 p. $1.00. D 2.8:M58/969

A handy traveler's guide which serves as an aid in the Middle Eastern countries. Gives descriptions of the land and peoples, and simple phrases in Arabic, Hebrew and Persian. Includes a brief bibliography of more extensive guides.

PAKISTAN

171. U.S. Department of the Air Force. Air University Library. **Pakistan, Selected Unclassified References.** Maxwell Air Force Base, Ala., Air University,

1968. 25 p. Issuing Agency. D 301.26/11:77(rev.), pt.1

This is an alphabetical listing of references to books and periodical articles on Pakistan arranged under the headings of economics, foreign relations, politics, military affairs, and psycho-social aspects. Not annotated or indexed. Part 2 of this bibliography is classified and can only be used by persons with the proper security clearance.

THAILAND

172. U.S. Department of the Army. **Area Handbook for Thailand.** By Harvey H. Smith and others. Prep. by Foreign Area Studies, American University. Washington, GPO, 1968. 558 p. Illus. $4.00. LC Card No. 74-600099. D 101.22:550-53

One of a series of handbooks designed for military and other personnel who need a convenient compilation of basic facts on specific countries. Provides a comprehensive survey of the society of Thailand. A brief, quick reference summary in the front gives basic facts on the country, government, population, climate, etc. and cites recent legislation in regard to citizenship and other vital areas. Arranged in four major sections: Social, Political, Economic and National Security, with numerous chapter divisions on specific topics. Additional materials include a bibliography, a glossary and an index.

VIETNAM

173a. U.S. Department of the Air Force. Air University Library. **Asia, Southeastern (Excluding Vietnam), Selected Unclassified References.** Comp. by Gaye Byars. Maxwell Air Force Base, Ala., Air University, 1968. 31 p. Issuing Agency. D 301.26/11:156(rev.), supp.5, pt.1

An alphabetical listing of references to books and periodical articles on Burma, Cambodia, Indonesia, Laos, Malaysia, Singapore, Philippines, and Thailand, covering the following subjects: communism, economic aspects, military aspects, politics and government, psycho-social aspects, U.S. policy. Not annotated or indexed.

173b. U.S. Department of the Air Force. Air University Library. **Asia, Southeastern (Vietnam), Selected Unclassified References.** Comp. by Gaye Byars. Maxwell Air Force Base, Ala., Air University, 1968. 56 p. Issuing Agency. D 301.26/11:156(rev.), supp.5, pt. 2

Covers the economic aspects, military aspects (including numerous specific topics), politics and government, U.S. policy, and world opinion.

Part 3 of this bibliography is classified and can only be used by persons with the proper security clearance.

174. U.S. Agency for International Development. **Vietnam, a Bibliography.** Prep. by Judith W. Heaney. Washington, Agency for International Development, 1968. 25 p. Issuing Agency. LC Card No. 70-600671. S 18.21/2:V67

Lists works alphabetically by author under the following headings:

(1) general works; (2) physical and cultural setting; (3) South Vietnam's history prior to 1954; (4) South Vietnam between 1954 and 1963; (5) South Vietnam since 1963; (6) economy; (7) government and politics; (8) North Vietnam and Communist Insurgency Warfare; (9) fiction, the arts, and travel. A few brief annotations but no index.

EUROPE

GENERAL WORKS

175. U.S. Department of the Air Force. Air University Library. **Europe, Western, Selected References.** Comp. by Melrose Bryant. Maxwell Air Force Base, Ala., Air University, 1968. 124 p. Issuing Agency. D 301.26/11:188, supp.4, pt.1

Contains general information for the continent on the following subjects: economic aspects, military aspects, politics and government, psycho-social aspects, science and technology. The same subject divisions are used under the following countries or areas: Austria, Benelux, France, West Germany, Great Britain, Greece, Ireland, Italy, Portugal, Scandinavia, Spain and Switzerland. Not annotated or indexed.

Part 2 of this bibliography is classified and can only be used by persons with the proper security clearance.

CZECHOSLOVAKIA

176. U.S. Library of Congress. **Czechoslovakia, A Bibliographical Guide.** By Rudolf Sturm. Washington, GPO, 1968. 157 p. $1.00. LC Card No. 68-60019. LC 35.2:C99/2

Includes materials which will be used primarily by "librarians building their collections relating to Czechoslovakia, specialists dealing with the area in depth; and . . . general readers with only occasional and less specialized interests."

Part I is a discussion of the publications under form and subject headings (e.g. bibliographies, social conditions) with numbers which refer to Part II, an alphabetical listing. NUC symbols are provided to show in which libraries the publications may be found. Books published earlier than 1914 were not included.

SOVIET UNION

177. U.S. Department of the Army. **USSR Strategic Survey Bibliography.** Washington, GPO, 1969. 238 p. $5.00. LC Card No. 77-601689. D 101.22: 550-6

Contains abstracts of unclassified publications and is "intended to serve both the needs of the experts with responsibility for policy and strategy as well as those who simply need descriptive information about the Soviet Union." The 1000 items included cover the period from the last quarter of 1963 through August 1968. Divided into four major sections: (1) Introduction: Fifty Years of Soviet Power; An Overview; (2) National Policy, Strategy and Objectives;

(3) The Soviet Nation: The Spectrum of Politics, Sociology and Economics; and (4) Aids to Further Research on the Soviet Union (which lists reference books, primarily bibliographies). Annotations are lengthy and descriptive. Includes maps.

178. U.S. Library of Congress. **Half Century of Soviet Serials, 1917-68: A Bibliography and Union List of Serials Published in the USSR.** Comp. by Rudolf Smits. Washington, GPO, 1968. 2 v. $16.00. LC Card No. 68-62169. LC 29.2:So8/3/v. 1 & 2

Includes all known serial publications appearing in the Soviet Union at regular or irregular intervals since 1917, in all except oriental languages. Serials published outside the Soviet Union and newspapers are excluded. Symbols of libraries in the U.S. and Canada in which a title is known to be represented have been taken from the 1967 edition of **Union List of Serials,** from **New Serials Titles** or from catalog cards sent to the Slavic Union Catalog by cooperating libraries. Contains 29,761 entries arranged alphabetically by title (or issuing body when the title is not distinctive). For each entry it gives the language (when not Russian) in parentheses following the title, place of publication, year the serial began publication, name of issuing body (for title entries), frequency, miscellaneous remarks concerning titles changes, suspensions of publication for periods of time, etc., and data regarding library holdings in the U.S. and Canada. Over 28,000 cross references are also provided. Includes some serials which the Library of Congress has classified separately as monographs with a special note to that affect.

179. U.S. Library of Congress. **Monthly Index of Russian Accessions.** Washington, GPO, 1948-70. Monthly. $23.00/yr. LC Card No. 48-46562. LC 30.10:vols.

This series which began in 1948 lists Russian language books and periodicals (including those published in and out of the Soviet Union) received by the Library of Congress. Includes monographs and periodicals in separate sections with an alphabetical subject index (in English) to both sections. Contains an annual author index.

180. U.S. Library of Congress. **USSR and Eastern Europe, Periodicals in Western Languages.** Comp. by Paul L. Horecky and Robert G. Carlton. 3rd ed., rev. and enl. Washington, GPO, 1968. 89 p. $0.55. LC Card No. 68-60045. LC 35.2:P41/967

Primarily current periodicals in West European languages or English published in or dealing with Albania, the Baltic countries, Bulgaria, Czechoslovakia, Hungary, Poland, Rumania, the Soviet Union, and Yugoslavia. Includes "a highly selective list of periodicals which, though now defunct, are thought to be of continuing research value to students of this area." Alphabetical by countries. Frequency, cost, publisher and brief description given for each. Index of titles and issuing organizations, plus an index by broad subject headings.

OCEANIA

PHILIPPINES

181. U.S. Department of the Army. **Area Handbook for the Philippines.** By Frederic H. Chaffee and others. Prep. by Foreign Area Studies, American University. Washington, GPO, 1969. 413 p. Illus. $3.50. LC Card No. 78-601326. D 101.22:550-72

One of a series of handbooks designed for military and other personnel who need a convenient compilation of basic facts on specific countries. Provides a comprehensive survey of the society of the Philippines. A brief, quick reference summary in the front gives basic facts on the country, government, population, climate, etc. and cites recent legislation in regard to citizenship and other vital areas. Arranged in four major sections: Social, Political, Economic and National Security, with numerous chapter divisions on specific topics. Additional materials include a bibliography, a glossary and an index.

STATISTICS

GENERAL WORKS

182. U.S. Bureau of the Census. **Foreign Statistical Publications Accessions List.** Washington, Bureau of the Census, 1969. 4 issues. Issuing Agency. LC Card No. 49-3797. C 3.199:(date)

UNITED STATES

BIBLIOGRAPHIES

183. U.S. Bureau of the Census. **Bureau of the Census Catalog.** Washington, GPO, 1969. Quarterly & monthly issues. $2.25/yr. LC Card No. 47-46253. C 3.163/3:1969

Issued quarterly with monthly supplements and annual cumulations. Includes unpublished materials which are available on punched cards or computer tapes.

184. U.S. Bureau of the Census. **Census Bureau Methodological Research, Annotated List of Papers and Reports.** Washington, GPO, 1968– . Annual. $0.35. LC Card No. 68-7966. C 3.163/4:M56/yr.

First edition (1968) covers the years 1963-66; two subsequent editions cover 1967 and 1968. This is "a list of staff papers and publications on Bureau of the Census methodological research." The series was initiated to inform the Census staff of research being done, and to "provide access to documents from other relevant research and encourage wider dissemination of reports on research developments." Arranged by types of research with an author index.

185. U.S. Public Health Service. **Marriage and Divorce, a Bibliography of Statistical Studies.** Washington, Public Health Service, 1969. 9 p. Issuing Agency. LC Card No. 79-604103. FS 2.121:M34/969

This bibliography was compiled to "provide a guide to quantative research studies on marriage and divorce." Includes only those publications which utilized marriage and divorce statistics, or included theories and findings which could be tested by analyses of quantative data, or which are reports of quantitative research, or are bibliographies of reports of recent literature, or are statistical treatments of marriage and divorce. Arranged under broad subject headings but not annotated or indexed.

COMPENDIUMS

186. U.S. Bureau of the Census. **1970 Census User Guide (Second Draft).** Washington, GPO, 1969. 267 p. Illus. Issued with perforations. $5.25 (including supplements issued over six month periods). C 3.3/2:970

This second draft furnishes potential users of census data with an overview of what the census is about, and the scope of the next decennial census to be taken April 1, 1970. The Guide contains a description of each data product and service to be available from the 1970 Census data base, and summary information is given on subject content, geographic detail, etc. Information is given on how to obtain 1970 census summary computer tapes and how format can be rearranged to best suit use of individual groups. Prepared by the Data Access and Use Laboratory.

187. U.S. Bureau of the Census. **Pocket Data Book, U.S.A., 1969.** Prep. under the supervision of William Lerner. 2nd ed. Washington, GPO, 1969. 360 p. $2.75. LC Card No. A66-7638. C 3.134/3:969

This pocket-size quick statistical reference source is in its second biennial edition. Part one, Summary, contains 31 charts and easy-to-read graphs which summarize the data in part two. Part two, Tables, includes 29 tables on population, vital statistics, labor, welfare, finance, etc., covering the same areas as the **Statistical Abstract.** Both tables and graphs are simplified, some are in color, and are easy to read and use. The data are condensed from the **Statistical Abstract** and cites general source of information.

188. U.S. Bureau of the Census. **Statistical Abstract of the United States: 1969.** 90th Annual ed. Prep. under the supervision of William Lerner. Washington, GPO, 1969. 1032 p. $5.75. LC Card No. 4-18089. C 3.134:969

Published annually since 1878, this handy and indispensable volume is the standard summary of statistics on the social, political and economic organization of the United States. It also serves as a guide to other statistical publications and sources. Summarizes data from governmental and private agencies. Emphasis is on national data but international as well as regional and state tables are included.

This 90th annual edition represents a review and updating of more than 1300 tables, charts and text notes presenting "data for the most recent year or period available during the early part of 1969." 61 tables found in the 1968 edition are omitted and 56 entirely new tables are added to the 1969 edition.

The new tables are located in 23 sections and cover a variety of topics. The Metropolitan Area Statistics, first added to the 1967 edition, has been updated for the third consecutive year.

The appendix contains: A Guide to Sources of Statistics, Publications of Recent Censuses, and A Guide to State Statistical Abstracts.

Thoroughly indexed.

189. U.S. Department of Housing and Urban Development. **Statistical Yearbook, 1967.** Washington, GPO, 1969. 382 p. $3.00. LC Card No. 68-62733. HH 1.28:105

"The second HUD **Statistical Yearbook** brings together comprehensive and detailed data on program and financial operations of the Department and related statistical information on housing and urban development activity." One section, "General Statistics," contains information published by other government departments and private sources. The other sections contain HUD data. At the beginning of each section is an index listing each table and its page location. This is a major source of statistical information on housing and urban affairs.

190. U.S. Immigration and Naturalization Service. **Annual Indicator of In-Migration into the United States of Aliens in Professional and Related Occupations, Fiscal Year 1968.** Prep. by the Staff for the Council on International Education and Cultural Affairs. Washington, GPO, 1969. 177 p. $1.75. LC Card No. 68-67277. J 21.15:968

The Annual Indicator is a continuation and expansion of the series of charts originally included in **Some Facts and Figures on the Migration of Talent and Skills** (Dept. of State, 1967). The statistics cover all major countries.

191. U.S. Public Health Service. Division of Vital Statistics. **Vital Statistics of the United States, 1967: Volume I—Natality; Volume II—Mortality, part A & B.** Washington, GPO, 1969. 3 vols. $4.00 (Vol. I), $5.50 (Vol. II, Part A) and $6.50 (Vol. II, Part B). FS 2.112:967

Published annually since 1937. Volume I contains three sections: natality rates and characteristics, local area statistics and technical appendix. Volume II, Part A, Mortality, is in six sections: general, infant, fetal, accidental, life tables, and a technical appendix. Volume II, Part B covers geographic details of mortality. The technical appendixes discuss sources, classification, and quality of statistics reported in the volumes as well as population tables for computing vital rates.

DIRECTORIES

192. U.S. Public Health Service. National Vital Statistics Division. **Where to Write for Birth and Death Records.** Washington, GPO, 1968. 11 p. $0.15. LC Card No. 59-60613. FS 2.102:B53/3/968

Gives addresses for obtaining birth and death records, the cost of the records and special remarks which tell such things as gaps in the records. Arranged alphabetically by state and territory. Provides a listing of other types of records which may prove birth facts, and explains the different types of birth certificate records issued. Includes instructions for ordering.

193. U.S. Public Health Service. National Vital Statistics Division. **Where to Write for Divorce Records: United States and Outlying Areas.** Washington, GPO, 1968. 7 p. $0.10. LC Card No. 59-60669. FS 2.102:D64/968

"An official record of every divorce or annulment of marriage should be available in the place where the event took place." Lists addresses and cost of copies of records.

ECONOMICS & BUSINESS

GENERAL WORKS

194. U.S. Department of Commerce. **Dictionary of Economic and Statistical Terms.** Prep. by James M. Howell, Donna J. Tolli and Dawn Nelson. Washington, GPO, 1969. 73 p. $1.25. LC Card No. 70-605347. C 1.2:Ec7/7

Prepared as an aid to understanding and using the publications and press releases of the Bureau of the Census and the Office of Business Economics, this dictionary is designed to serve both as a convenient reference for those who are already familiar with the concepts and terms used in the publications of these agencies and as an introductory manual for those with a limited background in economic statistics. It is divided into four parts: (1) National Income and Product Accounts; (2) Balance of Payments Accounts; (3) Economic and Statistical Indicators; and (4) Economic and Statistical Terms, with a single alphabetical index to terms in all four parts.

195. U.S. Office of Economic Opportunity. **Catalog of Federal Domestic Assistance.** Washington, OEO, 1969. 610 p. Issuing Agency. LC Card No. 74-600920. PrEx 10.2:P94/969

This catalog supersedes the **Catalog of Federal Assistance Programs,** (June 1967).

Provides "a description of the federal government's domestic programs to assist the American people in furthering their social and economic progress." The summary description for each program provides specific information, its nature and purpose, availability, authorizing legislation and the administering agency, and where additional information may be found. Programs are arranged alphabetically by departments. Thoroughly indexed.

COMMERCE & FOREIGN TRADE

196. U.S. Bureau of the Census. **Guide to Foreign Trade Statistics.** Washington, GPO, 1969. 139 p. $1.25. LC Card No. 66-62924. C 3.6/2:F76/969

"Intended to serve as a guide to the various sources of foreign trade statistics, to inform users of the content and arrangement of data . . . and to assist in the location of particular information and make it possible to utilize the sources to better advantage." Explains the coverage of statistics with sample illustrations of the content and arrangement of material in individual publications and foreign trade reports.

197. U.S. Bureau of the Census. **U.S. Foreign Trade Statistics Classifications and Cross Classifications.** Washington, Bureau of the Census, 1965-68. 7 v. Issuing Agency. C 3.150:(Letters)

A necessary series for anyone involved in foreign trade. Includes the following schedules:

B—Statistical Classification of Domestic and Foreign Commodities Exported from the United States (1965)

C—Classification of Country Designations Used in Compiling the United States Foreign Trade Statistics (1967)

D—Code Classification of the United States Customs Districts and Ports (1967)

K—Code Classification of Foreign Ports by Geographic Trade Area and Country (1968)

P—Commodity Classification Reporting Shipments from Puerto Rico to the United States (1967)

R—Code Classification and Definitions of Foreign Trade Areas (1967)

W—Statistical Classification of U.S. Waterborne Exports and Imports (1966)

198. U.S. Bureau of International Commerce. **Semi-annual Checklist, Bureau of International Commerce, International Business Publications.** Washington, GPO, 1969. 21 p. Illus. Issuing Agency. C 42.15:C41/969-2

This checklist is issued twice each year listing available publications. Contents cover Trade Lists, Market Share Reports, World Trade Directories, Export-Import Summaries, etc. There is a list by country of all publications in the checklist.

199. U.S. Bureau of International Commerce. **Sources on American Firms for International Buyers.** Rev. ed. Washington, GPO, 1968. 35 p. $0.20. LC Card No. 63-65026. C 42.2:Am3/968

A bibliography which directs businessmen who need information on American companies to the proper sources. Complete bibliographical data provided, usually with price. Limited to those directories or guides which are "revised periodically or kept up to date with supplements."

200. U.S. Department of Commerce. **Industrial Processes, Selected Bibliographic Citations Announced in U.S. Government Research and Development Reports, 1966.** Washington, Department of Commerce, 1968. 48 p. Issuing Agency. C 1.54:In2

Accumulation of 1966 citations in **U.S. Government Research and Development Reports** on industrial processes. Entries are arranged by accession numbers. Detailed annotations. No index.

201. U.S. Department of Commerce. **United States Department of Commerce Publications, 1968 Supplement, Catalog and Index.** Comp. by Guy F. Glossbrenner. Washington, GPO, 1969. 66 p. $0.35. LC Card No. 52-60731.

202. U.S. Department of Commerce. **U.S. Department of Commerce Periodicals to Aid Businessmen.** Rev. ed. Washington, GPO, 1969. 40 p. Issuing Agency.

Lists a wide variety of business-oriented periodicals with brief annotations covering frequency and contents.

CONSUMERS

203. U.S. President. **Consumer Education: Bibliography.** Prep. for the President's Committee on Consumer Interests, Washington, D.C. by the Yonkers Public Library, Yonkers, N.Y. Washington, GPO, 1969. 170 p. $0.65. LC Card No. 77-601488. PR 36.8:C76/B47

This resource materials bibliography prepared for consumer education teachers lists 2000 books, booklets, pamphlets, films and filmstrips in the Field of consumer interests and education. Items omitted include those which appear in "obvious sources such as university extension publications." Arranged under 13 broad categories such as: consumer classics, money management, taxation, fraud. Indicates form and general level, e.g., "book, adult" and provides very brief annotations for most entires. Entries are by title and give author, date, publisher, pages and price. Documents number and price given for government publications. Not indexed.

BUSINESS & INDUSTRY

GENERAL WORKS

204. U.S. Senate. **Handbook for Small Business; a Survey of Small Business Programs of the Federal Government.** Washington, GPO, 1969. 200 p. $1.75. 91-1:Sen.Doc.45

"Designed to gather, into one comprehensive volune, information on programs of the federal government beneficial to small business." Describes the activities of various agencies pertaining to small business and provides an over-all view of the major areas of governmental help to small business.

205. U.S. Small Business Administration. **Survey of Federal Government Publications of Interest to Small Business.** Comp. by Elizabeth G. Janezeck. 3rd ed. Washington, GPO, 1969. 85 p. $0.45. LC Card No. 74-604710. SBA 1.18/2:G74/969

This bibliography is "intended to help small business owners in selecting publications from the many publications issued each year by various departments . . . and other administrative arms of the Federal Government." The first section lists materials under subjects, the second by issuing agency.

DIRECTORIES

206. U.S. Economic Development Administration. **Directory of Approved Projects.** Washington, EDA, 1969. 4 issues. Issuing Agency. C 46.19/2:969

Lists all projects, by states, approved for EDA assistance under Public Law 89-136, passed August 26, 1965. Approved projects are listed and described in tabular form: (1) applicant's name, location, project description and identification number; (2) congressional district number; (3) date approved; (4) Public Works grants; (5) business loans; (6) working capital guaranteed; (7) planning grant; (8) technical assistance; (9) EDA grant; (10) regular grant; and (11) funds distributed.

207. U.S. Economic Development Administration. **Directory of Private Pro-grams for Minority Business Enterprise.** 1st ed. Prep. for the Office of Minority Business Enterprise. Washington, Department of Commerce, 1969. 58 p. Issuing agency. LC Card No. 72-603592. C 1.56:969

Lists private programs, in 11 selected cities of the United States, which were organized to aid minority businessmen. Within each city, this list provides names, addresses, directors' names and descriptions of local organizations. National organizations are listed in a separate chapter. Although limited in coverage, it would be a useful source for these eleven cities: Atlanta, Baltimore, Cleveland, Detroit, Durham, Los Angeles, Newark, Philadelphia, Pittsburgh, San Antonio and Washington.

208. U.S. House of Representatives. Select Committee on Small Business. Subcommittee No. 1. **Tax Exempt Foundations: Their Impact on Small Business.** Washington, GPO, 1968. 813 p. $6.50. Y4.Sm1:T19/2/v.2

Lists over 30,000 tax exempt foundations registered with the Internal Revenue Service. Arranged first by IRS District numbers, then alphabetically by name of the foundation. Gives addresses.

209. U.S. Travel Service. **Plant Tours for International Visitors to the United States.** Washington, GPO, 1969. 167 p. $1.00. LC Card No. 66-60936. C 47.2:P69/969

"As part of the program to welcome international visitors to the United States, the U.S. Travel Service has compiled a listing of plant tours." All information was supplied by the Travel Service liaison officers in the various states. Arranged alphabetically by state, city and name of the plant. A number beside each entry keys that entry to the Industrial Classification Index located at the front. Each entry gives a brief description of the plant's operation, tells when tours are conducted, how long they last and any specific rules.

STATISTICS

210. U.S. Bureau of the Census. **List of Materials Consumption Items.** Washington, GPO, 1969. 304 p. $2.25. LC Card No. 77-60118. C 3.24/2:M41/2/967

"Lists materials for which data on consumption were collected in the 1967 Census of Manufactures and Mineral Industries." Lists the materials, census codes and unit of measure for quantities. Does not present the statistics but only a list of the materials for which data were collected.

211. U.S. Business and Defense Services Administration. **Industry Profiles, 1958-67.** 3rd ed. Washington, GPO, 1969. 184 p. $1.50. C 41.2:In2/25/958-67)

Provides statistical data on the economic development of 418 manufacturing industries from 1958 to 1967. It was designed to "provide users of industrial data with a convenient single source of comparable basic industry statistics." For each of the 418 industries, 16 basic statistical series provide data on employment, payrolls, capital expenditures, manhours, etc. Arranged by four digit SIC numbers. No subject index. Five supplementary tables give related statistical information. A chapter entitled, "Industry Title and Description," explains what is included within each SIC number.

212. U.S. Business and Defense Services Administration. **U.S. Industrial Outlook, 1970.** Washington, GPO, 1969. 486 p. $4.75. LC Card No. 60-60662. C 41.42/3:970

"Presents narrative and statistical trend analyses on an industry-by-industry basis for major areas in the U.S. economy." Each industry section contains information on recent developments, effects of new technology, international trade and prospects for the coming year. Three appendixes provide additional statistical information. Includes a detailed subject index.

213. U.S. Federal Power Commission. **Statistics of Interstate Natural Gas Pipeline Companies, 1968.** Washington, GPO, 1969. 140 p. $1.25. FP 1.21: 197

Contains financial and operating statistics compiled from the annual reports filed with the Federal Power Commission by 80 Class A and B interstate natural gas pipeline companies.

214. U.S. Office of Business Economics. **Business Statistics; 1969 Statistical Supplement to the Survey of Current Business.** Washington, GPO, 1969. 400 p. $3.00. C43.8/4:969

This basic reference volume is issued biennially as a supplement to the monthly **Survey of Current Business,** and is designed to provide historical perspective to the numerous economic statistics provided in that periodical. This volume provides data for approximately 1500 series from 1939 through 1968. Materials are easy to locate through use of the edge index on the back cover and the detailed subject index. An appendix provides monthly or quarterly data for approximately 350 of the more important economic series.

AGRICULTURAL INDUSTRY

215. U.S. Economic Research Service. **Agriculture in the European Economic Community, An Annotated Bibliography, 1958-66.** By Brian D. Hedges and Reed F. Friend. Washington, GPO, 1968. 77 p. Issuing Agency. LC Card No. Agr 68-127. A 93.21/2:213

An "annotated list of over 300 publications dealing with various aspects of agriculture in the European Economic Community," with a major emphasis on "studies dealing with factors affecting the demand, supply and trade of agriculturals commodities." Includes studies in English, French, German, Italian, Dutch and Spanish. Four main sections: (1) Methodology, Statistics and Projections; (2) International Trade; (3) The Agricultural Situations; and (4) Commodity Studies. Entries are alphabetical under subheadings. Not indexed.

216. U.S. Economic Research Service. **Economics of Agriculture, Reports and Publications Issued or Sponsored by USDA's Economic Research Service, October 1966-September 1967.** Comp. by Irene L. Hardaway. Washington, Economic Research Service, 1968. 17 p. Issuing Agency. A 93.21:368

Updates ERS publication No. 350 (covering 1961-65) and No. 343 (Oct. 1965 to Sept. 1966).

"Intended to include citations for all published material of more than temporary interest regardless of the form in which it was published or current availability." Arranged by subjects under name of ERS divisions. No annotation; not indexed.

217. U.S. Bureau of International Commerce. Office of Commercial and Financial Policy. **Agribusiness Organization Directory.** Washington, Bureau of International Commerce, 1968. 50 p. Issuing Agency. LC Card No. 68-67333. C 42.2:Ag8/968

"A selected list of government and private organizations engaged in or concerned with international agribusiness." Lists U.S. government agencies, major foundations in international agribusiness and related fields, leaders in international agricultural programs in state universities and land grant colleges, financial organizations, and other international organizations. Addresses, objectives, sub-agencies, directors and their telephone numbers, and specific functions given for each.

CONSTRUCTION

218. U.S. General Services Administration. **Buildings Bibliography.** Washington, GPO, 1968. 79 p. $0.50. LC Card No. 68-62098. GS 1.17:B86

"This bibliography provides a basic, comprehensive reference and training tool for Government employees working in the broad areas of buildings design, construction, operation, and maintenance," but will also be useful for persons in this field regardless of employer. Arranged by subject; most entries are annotated. Indexes for subjects and personal and corporate names, referring to entry numbers. Includes a directory of publishers and a list of relevant periodicals.

FOOD INDUSTRY

219. U.S. Department of Agriculture. Consumer and Marketing Service. **Technical Terms of the Meat Industry.** Washington, Consumer and Marketing Service, 1968. 76 p. Issuing Agency. LC Card No. 74-601447. A 88.17/6:6

Defines technical terms of the meat industry and of meat inspectors in order to facilitate communications with those outside the field with whom they must work. Brief, clear definitions.

220. U.S. Bureau of Commercial Fisheries. **Cold Storage Warehouses Freezing and Storing Fishery Products.** Washington, Bureau of Commercial Fisheries, 1968. 15 p. Issuing Agency. I 49.28/2:4637

Lists warehouses alphabetically by states within geographic regions of the U.S. Includes names of companies and number of warehouses each company operates.

MINING

221. U.S. Bureau of Mines. **Dictionary of Mining, Minerals and Related Terms.** Comp. by Paul W. Thrush and the Staff of the Bureau of Mines. Washington, GPO, 1968. 1269 p. $8.50. LC Card No. 68-67091. I 28.2:D56

A standard reference source for the mining industry, comprehensive and authoritative. Contains about 55,000 terms and 150,000 definitions. Definitions are clear and concise. Includes technical and layman's terms. Excludes most petroleum, natural gas, and legal terminology, except the very general. Includes terminology from the entire English-speaking world, noting country of origin. Sources are given for each definition and a list of authorities and sources is included in the back of the book. Also contains a list of geological abbreviations.

222. U.S. Bureau of Mines. **List of Bureau of Mines Publications and Articles, January 1-December 31, 1968.** Washington, GPO, 1969. 119 p. $1.25. LC Card No. 61-64978. I 28.5:968

Contains both subject and author indexes to Bureau of Mines publications.

223. U.S. Bureau of Mines. **List of Bureau of Mines Publications on Oil Shale and Shale Oil, 1917-68.** Comp. by Marianne P. Rogers. Washington, GPO, 1969. 61 p. $0.65. LC Card No. 74-605044 I 28.17:8429

Lists and annotates publications from 1917 through 1968 by Bureau of Mines employees dealing with oil shale and shale oil. Entries are numbered and author index refers to entry numbers.

TEXTILE INDUSTRY

224. U.S. Business and Defense Services Administration. **Sources of Statistical Data, Textiles and Apparel, with List of Reference Sources.** By Barbara A. Steinbock and Thomas F. Stein. Washington, GPO, 1968. 31 p. $0.70. LC Card No. 68-67283. C 41.12:T31/968

Primary sources of statistical data on textiles and apparel are listed here by government agency and title. 'Secondary sources . . . generally have been omitted." Indexed by subject and title. Gives contents of the publications, frequency of publications, and price where available.

TRANSPORTATION INDUSTRY

225. U.S. Coast Guard. **Merchant Vessels of the United States, 1968 (Including Yachts).** Washington, GPO, 1969. 1521 p. $12.25. LC Card No. 76-605973. TD 5.12/2:968

Lists American merchant vessels and yachts which had uncancelled documents (i.e. register, license, or enrollment and licenses) on January 1, 1968. Provides the official number, signal and radio-call letters, rig information, name of vessel, symbols used for signal, classification, gross and net tonnage, dimensions, year of build and place, trade or business in which the vessel is engaged, horsepower, name of owner and home port for each.

226. U.S. National Archives and Records Service. **List of American-Flag Merchant Vessels that Received Certificates of Enrollment or Registry at the Port of New York, 1789-1867.** Comp. by Forrest R. Holdcamper. Washington, National Archives and Records Service, 1968. 2 v. (Special List, No. 22) 804 p. LC Card No. A68-7106. GS 4.7:22/v.1&2

Special lists are published by the National Archives and Records Service as part of their "records-description" program. These lists describe in detail the contents of groups of records, i.e. series of records that deal with the same subject or activity. This list contains names of "more than 26,000 American-flag merchant vessels that received certificates of enrollment or registry at the port of New York during the years 1789-1867." Arranged alphabetically by the name of the vessel and contains the following information for each: tonnage, rig, place and date built, and first New York certification. Index of compound names.

BUSINESS MANAGEMENT

GENERAL WORKS

227. U.S. National Aeronautics and Space Administration. **Management: Continuing Literature Survey, with Indexes; Selection of Annotated References to Unclassified Reports and Journal Articles Entering the NASA Information System.** Springfield, Clearinghouse, 1968— . Irregular. $3.00 each. LC Card No. 68-61755. NAS 1.21:7500(& nos.)

Three numbers of this series have been issued. The first [NASA SP-7500] includes NASA or NASA-generated materials published from 1962-67. The second [NASA SP-7500(01)] contains non-NASA materials published during the same period, and the third [NASA SP-7500(02)] contains all 1968 publications. Abstract section is first and contains abstracts from STAR (**Scientific and Technical Aerospace Reports**) and IAA (**International Aerospace Abstracts**) Second section contains three indexes; personal author, corporate author and subject. Indexes refer to entry numbers used in the first section. This publication is one of a series of technical and specialized bibliographies issued by NASA.

228. U.S. National Aeronautics and Space Administration. **Systems Approach to Management: An Annotated Bibliography with Indexes.** Springfield, Va., CFSTI, 1969. 62 p. $3.00. LC Card No. 75-603148. NAS 1.21:7501

229. U.S. Small Business Administration. **Distribution Cost Analysis.** Prep.

by Gorden Brunhild and Charles H. Sevin. Washington, SBA, 1969. 8 p. (Small Business Bibliography, no. 34). Issuing Agency. LC Card No. 70-600788. SBA 1.3:34

One in a series of bibliographies prepared for persons with specific interests in certain aspects of small business.

230. U.S. Small Business Administration. **Inventory Management.** By Donald F. Mulvihill. Washington, SBA, 1969. 8 p. (Small Business Bibliography, no. 75). Issuing Agency. LC Card No. 77-606965. SBA 1.3:75

One in a series of bibliographies prepared for persons with specific interests in certain aspects of small business.

231. U.S. General Accounting Office. **Glossary for Systems Analysis and Planning, Programming, Budgeting.** Washington, GPO, 1969. 72 p. Issuing Agency. LC Card No. 70-605043. GA 1.2:P69/969

This is a glossary of terms related to systems analysis, planning, programming and budgeting primarily for the federal government. "Because of the nontechnical nature of the definitions in this booklet users who require detailed technical information concerning terms are referred to the growing number of books which relate to the subjects involved." Definitions often include examples of the use of the terms in governmental context and cross references to related terms.

BOOKSTORES

232. U.S. Small Business Administration. **Bookstores.** Washington, SBA, 1968. 8 p. (Small Business Bibliography, no. 42). Issuing Agency. LC Card No. 68-62718. SBA 1.3:42/3

One in a series of bibliographies prepared for persons with specific interests in certain aspects of small business.

HARDWARE STORES

233. U.S. Small Business Administration. **Hardware Retailing.** Updated by Dorothy Ritter. Washington, SBA, 1968. 4 p. (Small Business Bibliography, no. 35). Issuing Agency. LC Card No. 72-600190. SBA 1.3:35

One in a series of bibliographies prepared for persons with specific interests in certain aspects of small business.

MACHINE SHOPS

234. U.S. Small Business Administration. **Machine Shops-Job Type.** By B. W. Niebel. Washington, SBA, 1968. 10 p. (Small Business Bibliography, no. 69). Issuing Agency. LC Card No. 68-62868. SBA 1.3:69

One in a series of bibliographies prepared for persons with specific interests in certain aspects of small business.

MEN'S AND BOYS' WEAR STORES

235. U.S. Small Business Administration. **Men's and Boys' Wear Stores.** By Don DeBolt. Rev. ed. Washington, SBA, 1968. 8 p. (Small Business Bibliography, no. 45). Issuing Agency. LC Card No. 68-62871. SBA 1.3:45

One in a series of bibliographies prepared for persons with specific interests in certain aspects of small business.

MOBILE HOMES & PARKS

236. U.S. Small Business Administration. **Mobile Homes and Parks.** By John M. Martin. Washington, SBA, 1969. 11 p. (Small Business Bibliography, no. 41). Issuing Agency. SBA 1.3:41/5

One in a series of bibliographies prepared for persons with specific interests in certain aspects of small business.

PAINTING & WALL DECORATING

237. U.S. Small Business Administration. **Painting and Wall Decorating.** By J. Wade Rice. Washington, SBA, 1968. 8 p. (Small Business Bibliography, no. 60). Issuing Agency. LC Card No. 68-61397. SBA 1.3:60/2

One in a series of bibliographies prepared for persons with specific interests in certain aspects of small business.

PERSONNEL MANAGEMENT

238. U.S. Civil Service Commission. **Personnel Literature.** Washington, Civil Service Commission, 1968-69. 12 issues. Issuing Agency. CS 1.62:v.27

Each monthly issue is a bibliography of selected books, pamphlets, periodical articles, unpublished dissertations, and other publications received by the Civil Service Commission Library during the previous month. "The material is selected on the basis of . . . its potential use for library research projects," and would also be useful for business or personnel managers. Arranged by subject with short descriptive annotations. No annual index.

239. U.S. Small Business Administration. **Personnel Management.** By Raymond O. Loen. Washington, SBA, 1969. 12 p. (Small Business Bibliography, no. 72). Issuing Agency. LC Card No. 74-605718. SBA 1.3:72

One in a series of bibliographies prepared for persons with specific interests in certain aspects of small business.

240. U.S. Small Business Administration. **Training Retail Salespeople.** By William B. Logan. Washington, SBA, 1968. 8 p. (Small Business Bibliography, no. 23). Issuing Agency. LC Card No. 70-600055. SBA 1.3:23

One in a series of bibliographies prepared for persons with specific interests in certain aspects of small business.

PHOTOGRAPHIC DEALERS & STUDIOS

241. U.S. Small Business Administration. **Photographic Dealers and Studios.** By William G. McClanahan. Washington, SBA, 1968. 8 p. (Small Business Bibliography, no. 64). Issuing Agency. LC Card No. 78-600432. SBA 1.3: 64/3

One in a series of bibliographies prepared for persons with specific interests in certain aspects of small business.

WOODWORKING SHOPS

242. U.S. Small Business Administration. **Woodworking Shops.** By William B. Lloyd. Washington, SBA, 1968. 11 p. (Small Business Bibliography, no. 46). Issuing Agency. SBA 1.3:46

One in a series of bibliographies prepared for persons with specific interests in certain aspects of small business.

VARIETY STORES

243. U.S. Small Business Administration. **Variety Stores.** By Sidney Hollander, Jr. Washington, SBA, 1969. 8 p. (Small Business Bibliography, no. 21). Issuing Agency. LC Card No. 77-603667. SBA 1.3:21/4

One in a series of bibliographies prepared for persons with specific interests in certain aspects of small business.

MARKETING

BIBLIOGRAPHIES

244. U.S. Business and Defense Services Administration. **Bibliography on Marketing to Low-Income Consumers.** Prep. in cooperation with the National Marketing Advisory Committee Task Force. Washington, GPO, 1969. 49 p. $0.55. LC Card No. 72-600495. C 41.12:M34/4

Includes materials which deal with the characteristics of the market system serving low income consumers and with programs designed to improve the market system. It was prepared, for the most part, by graduate students of the University of Minnesota, Clearinghouse for the Task Force on Commercial Services to Low-Income Urban Areas. 236 numbered entries are arranged in five groups: Characteristics and Buying Practices of Low-Income Consumers; Characteristics and Practices of Commercial Enterprises which Serve Low-Income Consumers; Conflicts and Problems in Low-Income Markets; Solving the Problems—Programs and Potential Solutions; and Miscellaneous. Provides full bibliographical citations. Includes government publications, articles from trade journals, conference proceedings, and a few monographs. Briefly annotated.

245. U.S. Business and Defense Services Administration. **Information Sources on Marketing New Products; Selections from Marketing Information Guide.** Washington, GPO, 1969. 24 p. Issuing Agency. C 41.12:M34/5

A handy reference source for publications in the field of developing and marketing new products as selected from the monthly **Marketing Information Guide.** Lists and annotates publications under the headings of (1) research; (2) planning and production, (3) patents and trademarks, (4) marketing techniques and (5) general information.

246. U.S. Business and Defense Services Administration. **Marketing Information Guide, An Annotated Bibliography.** Washington, GPO, 1959— . Monthly. $2.50/yr. LC Card No. 59-30923. C 41.11:v.nos. & nos.

Lists and annotates books, articles and other publications in the field of marketing distribution. Annotations describe the publications and give availability information. Each issue is indexed and the December issue contains a cumulative index for that year.

247. U.S. National Agricultural Library. **Marketing of Livestock, Meat, and Meat Products, 1962-June, 1967; a List of Selected References.** Comp. by Minnie N. Fuller and Betty B. Baxtresser. Washington, National Agricultural Library, 1968. 73 p. (Library List No. 92). Issuing Agency. LC Card No. Agr69-290. A 17.17:92

This bibliography was published in order to help research workers in the field of marketing livestock, meat and meat products get to the large body of publications in this field which previously were reported in a large number of scattered publications. It is highly selective dealing primarily with marketing economics. Arranged alphabetically under broad subject headings with author and subject indexes.

248. U.S. Small Business Administration. **Statistics and Maps for National Market Analysis.** By Thomas Semon, updated by Dorothy Ritter. Washington, SBA, 1969. 8 p. (Small Business Bibliography, no. 12). Issuing Agency. LC Card No. 70-605898. SBA 1.3:12

One in a series of bibliographies prepared for persons with specific interests in certain aspects of small business.

DIRECTORIES

249. U.S. Consumer and Marketing Service. **Federal-State Market News Reports, A Directory of Services Available.** Washington, Consumer and Marketing Service, 1968. 46 p. Issuing Agency. A 88.40/2:21/968

Contains "a listing of federal-state market news reports and offices that issue them, description of the market news leased wire network, and alphabetical tabulation of cities from which news reports are issued." Arranged by the eight subject areas of market news reports.

MAIL ORDER

250. U.S. Small Business Administration. **Selling by Mail Order.** By Richard D. Millican. Washington, SBA, 1968. 12 p. (Small Business Bibliography,

no. 3). Issuing Agency. SBA 1.3:3

One in a series of bibliographies prepared for persons with specific interests in certain aspects of small business.

RETAILING

251. U.S. Bureau of Labor Statistics. **Retail Prices of Food, 1964-68, Indexes and Average Prices.** Prep. by Kenneth V. Dalton. Washington, GPO, 1969. 62 p. $0.65. L 2.3:1632

Contains statistical data on retail food prices and indexes for the period 1964 to 1968 plus a discussion of price trends of major food groups, the method of calculating estimated average food prices for publication and a table of food item specifications.

252. U.S. Small Business Administration. **Discount Retailing.** By H. Nicholas Windeshausen. Washington, SBA, 1968. 7 p. (Small Business Bibliography, no. 68). Issuing Agency. SBA 1.3:68/3

One in a series of bibliographies prepared for persons with specific interests in certain aspects of small business.

253. U.S. Small Business Administration. **Retailing.** By William R. Davidson, Alton F. Doody and Daniel J. Sweeney. Washington, SBA, 1969. 15 p. (Small Business Bibliography, no. 10). Issuing Agency. LC Card No. 76-602809. SBA 1.3:10

One in a series of bibliographies prepared for persons with specific interests in certain aspects of small business.

MANUFACTURING

GENERAL WORKS

254. U.S. Bureau of the Census. **Alphabetic Index of Manufactured Products.** Washington, GPO, 1968. 100 p. $1.50. LC Card No. A68-7623.

"Provides a list of manufactured products, in alphabetic order, for use as an index to manufactured products coded to the full 7-digit in the 1967 Census of Manufacturers." Useful for those working with the product classification of the Standard Industrial Classification System.

255. U.S. Bureau of the Census. **Numerical List of Manufactured Products.** Washington, GPO, 1968. 305 p. $1.75. LC Card No. A68-7403. C 3.24/2: P94/4/967

"Contains principal products and services of the manufacturing industries in the United States for which data are being collected in the 1967 Census of Manufacturers." Serves as a coded reference list of the principal primary products of the manufacturing industries.

256. U.S. Department of Commerce. Business and Defense Services Administration. **Sources of Information on Containers and Packaging.** By Charles

H. Felton. Washington, GPO, 1969. 24 p. $0.25. C 41.2:C76/969

This publication is intended primarily for producers but contains information that may be of use to individuals or groups interested in packaging for protective or merchandising purposes. The publications and other sources of information listed here pertain to containers and packaging including their materials, manufacturing techniques, research and development, uses, distribution and production and trade statistics. Lists government and nongovernment publications, sources of technical information, directories, periodicals and trade associations.

STATISTICS

257. U.S. Bureau of the Census. **Annual Survey of Manufacturers, 1966.** Washington, GPO, 1969. 489 p. $6.25. LC Card No. 52-60884. C 3.24/9-2:966

This volume presents the results of the annual survey of manufacturers which is designed to yield estimates of general statistics for industry groups, individual industries, and geographic divisions including states, standard metropolitan statistical areas and large industrial counties. Chapters provide data on shipment values of classes of products, general statistics for industry groups, fuels and electrical energy used, value of fixed assets and expenditures for new plants and equipment. Six appendixes provide supplementary information such as an explanation of terms used, and provisions of the law relating to the annual survey.

258. U.S. Department of Agriculture. **Wood Used in Manufacturing Industries, 1965.** Washington, GPO, 1969. 101 p. $1.00. A 1.34:440

Presents statistical information on the volume of lumber, plywood, veneer, hardboard, particleboard, insulation board, and bolts used in manufacturing industries in 1965. It includes wood used in products made for sale; wood used for pallets, containers, skids, jugs, models, patterns, and flasks made and used in the same establishments; and wood used for dunnage, blocking and bracing.

LABOR & INDUSTRIAL RELATIONS

BIBLIOGRAPHIES

259. U.S. Department of Labor. **Labor Mobility, Selected References, Supplement to April 1967 Edition.** Washington, Department of Labor, 1969. 12 p. Issuing Agency. L 1.34:L11/6/supp.

An alphabetical listing of books and periodical articles on labor mobility. Not annotated or indexed.

260 U.S. Bureau of Labor Statistics. **Sources of Information on Labor in Japan.** Prep. by Theodore Bleecker. Washington, Bureau of Labor Statistics, 1968. 15 p. Issuing Agency. LC Card No. 79-600707. L 2.71:351

This bibliography is limited to sources of information on labor in Japan in the English language published from 1960 through early 1968. Materials are listed under subjects such as Labor-Management Relations and Labor Organizations, with some brief annotations. Not indexed.

CHRONOLOGIES

261. U.S. Department of Labor. **Important Events in American Labor History; Chronology 1778-1968.** Washington, GPO, 1969. 32 p. $0.25. LC Card No. L56-132. L 1.2:H62/2/778-968

A handy reference source for students and researchers, this chronology lists and describes major events in United States labor history.

DIRECTORIES

262. U.S. Bureau of Labor Statistics. **Directory of Industry Wage Studies and Union Scale Studies, 1960-October, 1968.** Washington, GPO, 1969. 21 p. $0.20. LC Card No. L61-66. L 2.34/2:W12/960-68

Lists the industry wage and union scale studies conducted by the Bureau of Labor Statistics from 1960 through October 1968. Industry wage studies provide information on the average straight time earnings of workers and union scale studies provide information on minimum wage scales and maximum schedules agreed on through collective bargaining. Studies are listed by type of industry.

263. U.S. Bureau of Labor Statistics. **Directory of Labor Organizations in the Republic of Korea.** Prep. in the Office of Foreign Labor and Trade. Washington, Bureau of Labor Statistics, 1969. 4 p. Issuing Agency. L 2.72/4:K84

This directory is a revision of Chapter 24 of the **Directory of Labor Organizations, Asia and Australasia, 1963.** It lists the labor organizations in Korea—their structures, principal officers, membership statistics, publications and international affiliations.

264. U.S. Bureau of Labor Statistics. **Directory of Labor Organizations in Malaysia.** Prep. in the Office of Foreign Labor and Trade. Washington, Bureau of Labor Statistics, 1969. 10 p. Issuing Agency. L 2.72/4:M29

This directory is a revision of Chapters 29 and 43 of the **Directory of Labor Organizations, Asia and Australasia, 1963.** It lists the labor organizations in Malaysia—their structures, principal officers, membership statistics, publications and international affiliations.

265. U.S. Bureau of Labor Statistics. **Labor Conditions and Labor Organizations in Australia.** Prep. in the Office of Foreign Labor and Trade. Washington, Bureau of Labor Statistics, (1967) 1969. 17 p. Issuing Agency. L 2.72/4:Au7

This directory is a revision of Chapter 3 of the **Directory of Labor Organizations, Asia and Australasia, 1963.** It lists the labor organizations—their structures, principal officers, membership statistics, publications and inter-national affiliations. A narrative summary of labor conditions is also included.

266. U.S. Bureau of Labor Statistics. **Labor Conditions and Labor Organiza-tions in New Zealand.** Prep. in the Office of Foreign Labor and Trade. Wash-ington, Bureau of Labor Statistics, (1967) 1969. 11 p. Issuing Agency. L 2.72/4:N42z

This directory is a revision of Chapter 36 of the **Directory of Labor Or-ganizations, Asia and Australasia, 1963.** It lists the labor organizations of New Zealand—their structures, principal officers, membership statistics, publications and international affiliations. A narrative summary of labor conditions is also included.

267. U.S. Bureau of Labor Statistics. **National Emergency Disputes; Labor Management Relations (Taft-Hartley) Act, 1947-68.** Washington, GPO, 1969. 90 p. $1.00. L 2.3:1633

Provides a chronological account of the unresolved issues that resulted in work stoppages of sufficient importance to warrant the use of the national emergency provision in the Labor Management Relations Act of 1947, of the efforts made by the parties and federal officials to resolve these differences, and of the actions of the Emergency Boards appointed to investigate the dis-putes and prepare findings.

STATISTICS

268a. U.S. Bureau of Labor Statistics. **Bureau of Labor Statistics Catalog of Publications, Periodicals, Bulletins, Reports, and Releases, January-June 1968.** Washington, GPO, 1968. 52 p. Issuing Agency. LC Card No. L48-22. L 2.34: 968/1

268b. U.S. Bureau of Labor Statistics. **Bureau of Labor Statistics Catalog of Publications, Periodicals, Bulletins, Reports, and Releases, July-December, 1968.** Washington, GPO, 1969. 45 p. Issuing Agency. LC Card No. L48-22. L 2.34: 968/2

This semi-annual catalog is a classified list of publications issued during the preceding six months. Brief summaries accompany many of the entries. Includes information for ordering publications. Updates the comprehensive **Publications of the Bureau of Labor Statistics, 1886-1967,** q.v.

269. U.S. Bureau of Labor Statistics. **Publications of the Bureau of Labor Statistics, 1886-1967.** Washington, GPO, 1968. 156 p. $1.00. L 2.3:1567

A numerical listing of the reports, bulletins, and current periodicals of the Bureau of Labor Statistics. Indexed by subject.

270. U.S. Bureau of Labor Statistics. **Directory of BLS Studies in Industrial Relations, 1954-69.** Rev. Washington, GPO, 1969. 26 p. Issuing Agency. LC Card No. L58-55. L 2.34/2:In2/2/954-69

271. U.S. Bureau of Labor Statistics. **Handbook of Labor Statistics, 1969.** Washington, GPO, 1969. 407 p. $3.75. LC Card No. 27-328. L 2.3:1630

The 1969 edition was compiled in the Office of Publications and makes available in one volume, the major series produced by the Bureau of Labor Statistics. Each table is complete historically, beginning with the earliest reliable and consistent data and running through the calendar year 1968. Related series from other governmental agencies and foreign countries are included. There are two major parts: Technical Notes describes major statistical programs and identifies the tables; and Tables, 162 tables arranged consecutively under 11 major subjects, e.g. Labor Force, Unemployment, Prices and Living Conditions. Every table is identified in the contents.

272. U.S. Bureau of Labor Statistics. **Major Programs, 1969.** Washington, GPO, 1969. 52 p. Issuing Agency. LC Card No. L60-83. L 2.87:969

Lists the principal programs in which the Bureau of Labor Statistics is currently engaged and groups major characteristics of the programs into related subject areas. In tabular form.

EMPLOYMENT

BIBLIOGRAPHIES

273. U.S. Bureau of Labor Statistics. **Bibliography of Manpower Projections for the North Central Region.** Washington, Bureau of Labor Statistics, 1968. 55 p. Issuing Agency. L 2.71/4:5

This is an annotated bibliography of publications concerning manpower projections for areas within the North Central region of the Bureau of Labor Statistics which includes the states of Illinois, Indiana, Kentucky, Michigan, Minnesota, Ohio and Wisconsin. The publications included are primarily studies published since 1962 and usually include projections of 10 to 15 years. Studies are listed by states and within states, alphabetically by personal or corporate authors. Annotations include a brief description of the nature of the study, a list of manpower projections it contains, and notes on the methodology. In addition, valuable information is contained in these appendixes: (1) Sources of Current Manpower Projects made by the U.S. Bureau of Labor Statistics; (2) Selected Sources of Federal Government and other Manpower and Population Projections; (3) Sources of Methodology for Making Manpower Projections; (4) Addresses of Organizations; and (5) Area Index.

274. U.S. Bureau of Labor Statistics. **Counselor's Guide to Manpower Information: An Annotated Bibliography of Government Publications.** Washington, GPO, 1968. 101 p. $1.00. L 2.3:1598

This bibliography was prepared to encourage wider use of the number of federal, state and local publications "which inform vocational counselors and others about trends and developments which have implications for career decisions." Publications are arranged within subject categories such as occupational and industry manpower literature, special groups in the labor force, sources of statistics, directories, bibliographies and catalogs. Appendix includes information on how to order publications.

275. U.S. Civil Service Commission. **Guide to Federal Career Literature.** Washington, GPO, 1969. 32 p. $0.55. CS 1.61:C18

Designed to serve as a convenient reference guide to federal recruiting literature, this directory contains brief descriptions of 246 publications from 46 different departments and agencies. The pamphlets and brochures listed represent only the principal publications used in nationwide recruiting for college entry-level positions.

276. U.S. Department of Health, Education and Welfare. **Career Development, Selected References.** Comp. by Dorothy M. Jones and Laura A. Miles. 2nd ed. Washington, Department of Health, Education and Welfare, 1968. 34 p. Issuing Agency. FS 1.18:C18/968

"The purpose of this bibliography is to bring to the attention of line and personnel managers at least part of the materials available in the general field of career development." Includes references on all aspects of employee development, including education in functional and professional abilities and training of clerical and other support-type personnel. Includes a separate section on bibliographies. Entries are briefly annotated. Not indexed.

DIRECTORIES

277. U.S. Civil Service Commission. **Directory of Interagency Boards of Civil Service Examiners.** Washington, GPO, 1969. 8 p. Issuing Agency. CS 1.2: In8/6

Lists Interagency Boards by states, with address, telephone number, and jurisdiction including counties from another state where applicable.

278. U.S. Civil Service Commission. **Federal Career Directory.** Washington, GPO, 1968. 87 p. $1.25. LC Card No. 63-60383. CS 1.7/4:C18/968

The 1968 edition of this directory, as well as earlier ones, was developed "in response to . . . the need for more specific information on Federal careers and basic entrance requirements." Part one concerns federal employment in general; Part two deals with federal agencies and their programs; Part three is an alphabetical list of federal career occupations describing each one and stating the nature of the work, qualifications and opportunities. Two indexes: a subject index of career opportunities described in part three and a subject index arranged under college majors.

279. U.S. Civil Service Commission. **Summer Jobs in Federal Agencies.** Washington, GPO, 1969. 35 p. Issuing Agency. CS 1.26:967/414/rev.2

Lists jobs available primarily for students, in 1970. Describes programs at various GS levels, and explains application procedures.

280. U.S. Bureau of Employment Security. **Directory of Local Employment Security Offices.** Washington, GPO, 1968. 83 p. Issuing Agency. L 7.68:968

Nearly 2,900 Bureau of Employment Security Offices arranged by state and city, giving complete address, local office number and type, purpose and occupational groups served by each local office. Special notations list restrictions and other unique features of each office. Includes a supplemental list of state employment security offices affiliated with the Bureau of Employment Security.

281. U.S. Department of Labor. **Job Guide for Young Workers, 1969-70 ed.** By Earl M. Sizemore and Bruce L. Dobbs. Washington, GPO, 1969. 200 p. $1.50. LC Card No. 76-605007. L 1.7/6:969-70

Designed especially for the high school graduate, this job guide lists names of people and places to go for information and advice concerning employment. It also discusses the benefits of further ecucation with information on financial aid for higher education. Includes a bibliography and an index by occupational titles.

282. U.S. Department of Labor. Training and Employment Service. **Guide to Local Occupational Information.** 3d ed. Washington, GPO, 1969. 144 p. Issuing Agency. LC Card No. 79-605048. L 34.8:Oc1

A directory of selected state employment services' studies "intended to provide current local occupational information for use in designing training programs for counseling in local public employment offices and schools and to offer individual job seekers and vocational counselors concrete information on job opportunities in specific occupations." Includes two basic types of local occupational information: Occupational Guides—concise summary of job duties and employment prospects for a single occupation or group of occupations in a state or particular area; Area Skill Surveys—comprehensive information on current employment and future requirements in individual labor areas.

RESEARCH

283. U.S. Bureau of Labor Statistics. **Summaries of Manpower Surveys and Reports for Developing Countries 1958-69.** Washington, GPO, 1969. 230 p. $1.75. L 2.3:1628

Contains quick reference to 226 Agency for International Development (AID) sponsored manpower reports and significant reports prepared by other organizations. Report summaries are arranged alphabetically by country in four groups: Africa, American Republics, East Asia and the Pacific, and Near East and South Asia. Summaries include statements on manpower administration and organizational machinery, mission accomplishments and major recommendations. Includes a brief list of selected readings.

284. U.S. Bureau of Employment Security. **Manpower and Operations Research Studies of the U.S. Employment Service and State Employment**

Services, 1958-1967: A Selected Bibliography. Prep. under the direction of Harold Kuptzin. Washington, Bureau of Employment Security, 1968. 145 p. Issuing Agency. LC Card No. 68-62863. L 7.61:E261

This bibliography was prepared to "acquaint researchers in the employment security system and in other groups with the full scope of [the Employment Service's] studies." Lists studies under appropriate subject headings with no descriptions or annotations.

285. U.S. Department of Labor. **Manpower Research Projects Sponsored by the Manpower Administration through June 30, 1969.** Washington, GPO, 1969. 296 p. Issuing Agency. LC Card No. 76-600453. L 1.39/6:969

Describes the content and status of all manpower research projects developed and administered by the Office of Manpower Research as of June 30, 1969. Lists active projects, those completed between July 1, 1968 and June 30, 1969, and reports completed from 1963-69. Provides detailed abstracts of each. Indexed by: (1) contractor and grantee institutions, (2) individuals associated with contracts or grants, (3) contract and grant numbers, and (4) research subjects.

STATISTICS

286. U.S. Bureau of Labor Statistics. **Employment and Earnings: States and Areas, 1939-68, Standard Industrial Classification.** Washington, GPO, 1969. 582 p. $5.25. L 2.3:1370-6

This is the seventh comprehensive historical reference volume of state and area employment and earnings statistics and replaces Bulletin 1370-5 (1939-67). This volume groups together information available under the Current Employment Statistics Program. A special section preceding the main body of statistics contains analytical and summary data. Includes employment data related to the nonfarm sector; excludes the self-employed and domestic workers. Presents detailed industry data on 242 major labor areas. Beginning with this edition, industry definitions are based on the Bureau of the Budget's 1967 **Standard Industrial Classification Manual.** A companion volume, **Employment and Earnings, United States, 1909-69** (Bulletin No. 1312-7), contains historical national statistics for individual non-agricultural industries, including monthly and annual data from the beginning date of each series through March 1969.

287. U.S. Bureau of Labor Statistics. **Employment and Earnings, United States, 1909-69.** Washington, GPO, 1969. 924 p. $5.75. L 2.3:1312-7

Contains historical statistics for individual nonagricultural industries, including monthly and annual data from the beginning date of each series through March 1969.

288. U.S. Bureau of Labor Statistics. **Manpower and Employment Statistics Publications of the Bureau of Labor Statistics; a Selected Bibliography.** Prep. by Owen E. Delap. Washington, Bureau of Labor Statistics, 1969. 32 p. Issuing Agency. LC Card No. 79-601763. L 2.34/2:M31

A selective list of publications of current interest published during the last five years. Limited to items from the Bureau of Labor Statistics.

289. U.S. Civil Service Commission. **Study of Employment of Women in the Federal Government, 1968.** Washington, GPO, 1969. 237 p. $2.00. CS 1.48: Sm62-04

Provides comprehensive statistics for evaluating the status of women in comparison to the total full-time white-collar federal workforce for the years 1966 and 1968. The purpose of the data is to supply a tool for use in assessing progress and in identifying areas where greater efforts must be made to assure equality of opportunity for women.

OCCUPATIONS

290. U.S. Bureau of Employment Security. **Selected Characteristics of Occupations by Worker Traits and Physical Strength.** Prep. by A.B. Eckerson, assisted by James E. Kelly. Washington, GPO, 1968. 156 p. $1.25. LC Card No. L66-20. L 7.2:Oc1/965/supp.2

Supplement 2 to the **Dictionary of Occupational Titles** (DOT).

Lists "occupational data by page numbers of worker trait groups. Page numbers refer to that section in Volume II of the DOT where worker trait groups are found." Under each worker trait group is a list of jobs requiring similar abilities and traits. This supplement differs from the first supplement (**Selected Characteristics of Occupations**) in arrangement. In the first supplement the same data are arranged by job codes. The columnar arrangement of this supplement provides the following data: (1) page number in volume 2 of the DOT, (2) DOT code numbers, (3) industry designation, (4) job title, (5) physical demands, (6) working conditions, and (7) training time. Three appendixes provide a complete explanation of the latter three columns. Especially useful for personnel managers.

FINANCE & BANKING

BIBLIOGRAPHIES

291. U.S. Small Business Administration. **Retail Credit and Collections.** Washington, SBA, 1969. 11 p. (Small Business Bibliography, no. 31). Issuing Agency. SBA 1.3:31/5

One in a series of bibliographies prepared for persons with specific interests in certain aspects of small business.

DIRECTORIES

292. U.S. Securities and Exchange Commission. **Directory of Companies Filing Annual Reports with the Securities and Exchange Commission.** Washington, GPO, 1969. 275 p. $2.25. LC Card No. 59-61379. SE 1.27:968

Lists companies which list stock on national exchanges and which have

registered under the Securities Act of 1934. Part one lists companies alphabetically by name with code numbers to industrial groups and Securities
Exchange docket numbers. Part two lists companies by nine major industrial
groups and subgroups.

STATISTICS

293. U.S. Federal Home Loan Bank Board. **Savings and Home Financing
Sourcebook, 1968.** Washington, Federal Home Loan Bank Board, 1969. 55 p.
Issuing Agency. LC Card No. 53-63519. FHL 1.11:968

Statistical information on institutions affiliated with the Federal Home
Loan Bank System and Federal Savings and Loan Insurance Corporation for
1968. Includes data on assets and liabilities, dividends, savings, interest rates,
mortgage activity, and residential construction.

294. U.S. Federal Reserve System Board of Governors. **Historical Chart Book,
1969.** Washington, Federal Reserve System, 1969. 123 p. $0.60. LC Card
No. 50-13379. FR 1.30/2:969

This annual publication contains long-range charts that supplement the
monthly **Federal Reserve Chart Book** on financial and business statistics. Covers
such topics as bank reserves and reserve bank credit, liquid assets and money
supply, commercial banks, government finance, business finance, agriculture,
consumer financing, and prices. Some charts show figures as far back as 1900.

INCOME TAX

295. U.S. Internal Revenue Service. **Farmer's Tax Guide.** 1970 ed. Washington, Internal Revenue Service, 1969. 47 p. Issuing Agency. LC Card No.
56-61352. T 22.19/2:F22/970

This booklet explains the special tax rules for income and self-employment
as they apply to farming.

296. U.S. Internal Revenue Service. **Statistics of Income, 1967: Individual
Income Tax Returns.** Washington, GPO, 1969. 259 p. Illus. $2.75. LC Card
No. 61-37567. T 22.35/2:In2/967

The data in this annual report is contained in ten sections. The first five
topical sections include text, tables and charts covering sources of income, deductions, tax rates, taxpayers over 65 and state and metropolitan area data.
Other sections are for explanation of terms, sources of data, historical summary,
forms samples and index. Similar publications are prepared for corporate, business and foreign income tax returns.

297. U.S. Internal Revenue Service. **Tax Guide for Small Business.** Washington, GPO, 1969. 158 p. $0.60. LC Card No. 57-60150. T 22.19/2:Sm1/970

This book provides details on Internal Revenue Service rules for small
business, individuals, sole proprietorships, partnerships and small corporations
concerning income, excise and employment taxes.

298. U.S. Internal Revenue Service. **Your Federal Income Tax.** 1970 ed. Washington, GPO, 1969. 160 p. $0.60. LC Card No. 44-40552. T 22.44:970

This publication is designed to help persons file federal income tax returns. It explains how to prepare forms, what exemptions and deductions are allowed, what income is taxable, how to determine income and deductions from investment properties, how to determine capital gains and losses, and other regulations. Examples are provided to make rules more easily understood and explanations are written clearly and concisely. A detailed index facilitates the use of this handy publication.

The Internal Revenue Service publications listed below contain information on special aspects of filing income tax returns. Although some of the information is contained in the above three publications, more details are given and therefore, these should also be consulted by those persons with specific tax problems or questions. All are based on the latest available court rulings and IRS interpretation and are arranged by Superintendent of Documents Classification numbers.

299. **Your Exemptions and Exemptions for Dependents.** Washington, GPO, 1969. 8 p. $0.10. T 22.44/2:501

300. **Deductions for Medical and Dental Expenses.** Washington, GPO, 1969. 8 p. $0.10. T 22.44/2:502

301. **Child Care and Disabled Dependent Care.** Washington, GPO, 1969. 11 p. $0.10. T 22.44/2:503/2

302. **Income Tax Deductions for Alimony Payments.** Washington, GPO, 1969. 8 p. $0.10. T 22.44/2:504/2

303. **Tax Withholding and Declaration of Estimated Tax.** Washington, GPO, 1969. 8 p. $0.10. T 22.44/2:505

304. **Computing Your Tax Under the Income Averaging Method.** Washington, GPO, 1969. 15 p. $0.15. T 22.44/2:506

305. **Tax Information on Scholarships and Fellowships.** Washington, GPO, 1969. 4 p. $0.10. T 22.44/2:507

306. **Tax Information on Educational Expenses.** Washington, GPO, 1969. 4 p. $0.10. T 22.44/2:508

307. **Tax Calendar and Check List for 1970.** Washington, GPO, 1969. 12 p. $0.15. T 22.44/2:509

308. **Information on Excise Taxes for 1970.** Washington, GPO, 1969. 11 p. $0.15. T 22.44/2:510

309. **Sales and Other Dispositions of Depreciable Property.** Washington, GPO, 1969. 11 p. $0.15. T 22.44/2:511

310. **Credit Sales by Dealers in Personal Property.** Washington, GPO, 1969. 8 p. $0.10. T 22.44/2:512

311. **Tax Information for Visitors to the United States.** Washington, GPO, 1969. 5 p. $0.05. T 22.44/2:513

312. **Foreign Tax Credit for U.S. Citizens and Resident Aliens.** Washington, GPO, 1969. 15 p. $0.15. T 22.44/2:514

313. **Withholding of Tax on Nonresident Aliens and Foreign Corporations.** Washington, GPO, 1969. 12 p. $0.15. T 22.44/2:515

314. **Tax Information for U.S. Government Civilian Employees Stationed Abroad.** Washington, GPO, 1969. 6 p. $0.10. T 22.44/2:516

315. **Social Security for Clergymen and Religious Workers.** Washington, GPO, 1969. 6 p. $0.10. (T 22.44/2:517

316. **Foreign Scholars and Educational and Cultural Exchange Visitors.** Washington, GPO, 1969. 34 p. $0.30. T 22.44/2:518

317. **United States Tax Guide for Aliens.** Washington, GPO, 1969. 36 p. $0.35. T 22.44/2:519/2

318. **Tax Information for American Scholars Abroad.** Washington, GPO, 1969. 6 p. $0.10. T 22.44/2:520

319. **Moving Expenses—Tax Information for Employees and Employers.** Washington, GPO, 1969. 4 p. $0.10. T 22.44/2:521

320. **Adjustments to Income for Sick Pay.** Washington, GPO, 1969. 12 p. $0.15. T 22.44/2:522

321. **Tax Information on Selling Your Home.** Washington, GPO, 1969. 11 p. $0.15. T 22.44/2:523

322. **Retirement Income and Retirement Income Credit.** Washington, GPO, 1969. 12 p. $0.15. T 22.44/2:524

323. **Taxable Income and Nontaxable Income.** Washington, GPO, 1969. 16 p. $0.15. T 22.44/2:525

324. **Income Tax Deductions for Contributions.** Washington, GPO, 1969. 11 p. $0.10. T 22.44/2:526/2

325. **Rental Income and Royalty Income.** Washington, GPO, 1969. 4 p. $0.10. T 22.44/2:527

326. **Information on Filing Your Tax Return.** Washington, GPO, 1969. 12 p. $0.15. T 22.44/2:528

327. **Other Miscellaneous Deductions.** Washington, GPO, 1969. 7 p. $0.10. T 22.44/2:529/2

328. **Tax Information on Deductions for Homeowners.** Washington, GPO, 1969. 8 p. $0.10. T 22.44/2:530

329. **Reporting Your Tips for Federal Income Tax Purposes.** Washington, GPO, 1969. 4 p. $0.10. T 22.44/2:531

330. **Tax Information for Students and Parents.** Washington, GPO, 1969. 7 p. $0.10. T 22.44/2:532

331. **Information on Self-Employment Tax.** Washington, GPO, 1969. 8 p. $0.10. T 22.44/2:533

332. **Depreciation, Investment Credit, Amortization, Depletion.** Washington, GPO, 1969. 19 p. $0.20. T 22.44/2:534

333. **Tax Information on Business Expenses.** Washington, GPO, 1969. 19 p. $0.20. T 22.44/2:535/2

334. **Losses from Operating a Business.** Washington, GPO, 1969. 7 p. $0.10. T 22.44/2:536

335. **Installment and Deferred-Payment Sales.** Washington, GPO, 1969. 15 p. $0.15. T 22.44/2:537

336. **Tax Information on Accounting Periods and Methods.** Washington, GPO, 1969. 10 p. $0.15. T 22.44/2:538

337. **Withholding Taxes from Your Employee's Wages.** Washington, GPO, 1969. 11 p. $0.15. T 22.44/2:539

338. **Tax Information on Repairs, Replacements and Improvements.** Washington, GPO, 1969. 4 p. $0.10. T 22.44/2:540

339. **Tax Information on Partnership Income and Losses.** Washington, GPO, 1969. 11 p. $0.15. T 22.44/2:541

340. **Corporations and the Federal Income Tax.** Washington, GPO, 1969. 22 p. $0.20. T 22.44/2:542

341. **Tax Information on the Sale of a Business.** Washington, GPO, 1969. 4 p. $0.10. T 22.44/2:543

342. **Sales and Exchanges of Assets.** Washington, GPO, 1969. 23 p. $0.20. T 22.44/2:544

343. **Income Tax Deductions for Interest Expense.** Washington, GPO, 1969. 7 p. $0.10. T 22.44/2:545/2

344. **Income Tax Deductions for Taxes.** Washington, GPO, 1969. 8 p. $0.10. T 22.44/2:546/2

345. **Tax Information on Disasters, Casualty Losses and Thefts.** Washington, GPO, 1969. 16 p. $0.15. T 22.44/2:547

346. **Tax Information on Deduction for Bad Debts.** Washington, GPO, 1969. 8 p. $0.10. T 22.44/2:548

347. **Condemnations of Private Property for Public Use.** Washington, GPO, 1969. 19 p. $0.20. T 22.44/2:549

348. **Tax Information on Investment Income and Expenses.** Washington, GPO, 1969. 22 p. $0.20. T 22.44/2:550

349. **Tax Information on Cost or Other Basic Assets.** Washington, GPO, 1969. 8 p. $0.10. T 22.44/2:551

350. **Recordkeeping Requirements and a Guide to Tax Publications.** Washington, GPO, 1969. 4 p. $0.10. T 22.44/2:552

351. **Highlights of 1969 Changes in the Tax Law.** Washington, GPO, 1969. 14 p. $0.10. T 22.44/2:553/2

352. **Tax Benefits for Older Americans.** Washington, GPO, 1969. 18 p. $0.20. T 22.44/2:554

353. **Community Property and the Federal Income Tax.** Washington, GPO, 1969. 7 p. $0.10. T 22.44/2:555

354. **Appeal Rights and Claims for Refund.** Washington, GPO, 1969. 4 p. $0.10. T 22.44/2:556

355. **How to Apply for Exemptions for an Organization.** Washington, GPO, 1969. 20 p. $0.20. T 22.44/2:557

356. **Tax Information for Sponsors of Contests and Sporting Events.** Washington, GPO, 1969. 4 p. $0.10. T 22.44/2:558

357. **Federal Tax Guide for Survivors, Executors and Administrators.** Washington, GPO, 1969. 22 p. $0.20. T 22.44/2:559/2

358. **Retirement Plans for Self-Employed Individuals.** Washington, GPO, 1969. 15 p. $0.15. T 22.44/2:560

359. **Valuation of Donated Property.** Washington, GPO, 1969. 15 p. $0.15. T 22.44/2:561

360. **Tax Information on Mutual Fund Distributions.** Washington, GPO, 1969. 12 p. $0.15. T 22.44/2:564

361. **Tax Information on the Interest Equalization Tax.** Washington, GPO, 1969. 22 p. $0.20. T 22.44/2:565

362. **Questions and Answers on Retirement Plans for the Self-Employed.** Washington, GPO, 1969. 8 p. $0.10. T 22.44/2:566

363. **Tax Advice on Civil Service Disability Retirement Payment.** Washington, GPO, 1969. 12 p. Issuing Agency. T 22.44/2:567

364. **Federal Tax Information for Civil Service Retirees.** Washington, GPO, 1969. 8 p. Issuing Agency. T 22.44/2:568

365. **Questions Asked by U.S. Taxpayers Abroad.** Washington, GPO, 1969. 12 p. $0.15. T 22.44/2:569

366. **Tax Guide for U.S. Citizens Employed in U.S. Possessions.** Washington, GPO, 1969. 14 p. $0.15. T 22.44/2:570

367. **Tax Sheltered Annuity Plans for Employees of Public Schools and Certain Tax-Exempt Organizations.** Washington, GPO, 1969. 19 p. Issuing Agency. T 22.44/2:571

INSURANCE AND RETIREMENT

368. U.S. Bureau of Labor Statistics. **Benefits for Active and Retired Workers Age 65 and Over.** Washington, GPO, 1968. 33 p. $0.40. L 2.3:1502-1

Supplement to Bulletin 1501 (**Digest of 100 Selective Health and Insurance Plans Under Collective Bargaining**). "This bulletin describes the health and life insurance benefits extended in early 1968 to retired workers age 65 and over and the health benefits for active workers in that age group." The plans cover many workers and therefore, this is representative of U.S. business in general. Index to companies with union acronyms, union identification chart and benefit summaries.

369. U.S. Children's Bureau. **Services for Children and Families Under the Social Security Acts Titles IV and V.** Washington, Children's Bureau, 1968. 19 p. Issuing Agency. FS 17.202:Se6

Programs are sponsored by the Children's Bureau as an outgrowth of the 1935 Social Security Act plus recent amendments. Explains who is eligible for funds. Gives explanations of criteria for grants and methods of distributing funds.

370. U.S. Department of the Army. **Handbook on Retirement Services for Army Personnel and their Families.** Washington, GPO, 1969. 161 p. $1.75. D 101.22:600-5/3

Thoroughly describes the status of retired army personnel and services available to them and their families. Includes sections on financial payments and benefits, rights and privileges, employment after retirement, and survivor benefits. Appendix lists veteran's regional offices, and includes sample letters and forms. Updated by **Retired Army Bulletin** published by the Adjutant General's Retired Activities Branch.

371a. U.S. Social Security Administration. **Directory of Medicare Providers of Services: Home Health Agencies.** 3rd ed. Washington, GPO, 1968. 155 p. $1.25. FS 3.51:968

371b. U.S. Social Security Administration. **Directory of Medicare Providers of Services: Hospitals.** 3rd ed. Washington, GPO, 1968. 291 p. $2.25. LC Card No. HEW67-113. FS 3.51/2:968

371c. U.S. Social Security Administration. **Directory of Medicare Providers of Services: Extended Care Facilities.** 3rd ed. Washington, GPO, 1968. 211 p. $1.75. LC Card No. HEW67-150. FS 3.51/3:968

371d. U.S. Social Security Administration. **Directory of Suppliers of Services: Independent Laboratories.** Washington, GPO, 1968. 147 p. $1.25. LC Card No. HEW68-12. FS 3.51/4:968

Listings of names and addresses of facilities which are participating in the Health Insurance for the Aged Program. All are arranged alphabetically by state, city and facility.

372. U.S. Social Security Administration. **Medicare, Bibliography of Selected References, 1966-67.** Washington, GPO, 1968. 88 p. $0.35. LC Card No. HEW68-56. FS 3.38:M46

Lists significant books, pamphlets, and journal articles on Medicare which were added to the Social Security Administration Library during the first year of Medicare (i.e. July 1, 1966 to June 30, 1967). Arranged by subject with author index. Separate lists of pertinent journals, indexing and abstracting services.

373. U.S. Social Security Administration. **Social Security Handbook.** 4th ed. Washington, GPO, 1969. 477 p. $2.25. FS 3.52:135

A handbook covering retirement, survivors, disability, and health insurance for the aged. The first edition was published in 1960, the second in 1963, and the third in 1966. This edition reflects provisions of the Social Security Act as amended through January 2, 1968, regulations issued and precedential case decisions. Twenty-five chapters cover all aspects of social security benefits. Brief table of contents is supplemented by separate chapter outlines and a detailed index.

374. U.S. Social Security Administration. **Your Social Security, Retirement, Survivors, and Disability Insurance.** Washington, GPO, 1969. 46 p. $0.15. FS 3.52:35/4

This is a handy reference source providing details on retirement, survivors, and disability payments; the amount of work required; hospital and medical insurance; trust funds, kinds of work covered; rights of appeal and other related subjects.

REAL ESTATE

375. U.S. Bureau of the Census. **New One-Family Homes Sold and For Sale, 1963-1967.** Prep. by the Construction Statistics Division in cooperation with the Department of Housing and Urban Development. Washington, GPO, 1969. 296 p. $4.75. LC Card No. 78-601125.

This is a historical supplement to the current data issued in the C25 series of Construction Reports, "Sales of New One-Family Homes," summarizing all significant data. Contains two major chapters, the United States and regions, and provides appendixes with descriptions of the survey and definitions.

376. U.S. Department of Housing and Urban Development. **Housing and Planning References.** Washington, GPO, 1969. 5 issues. $2.25/yr. HH 1.23/3: nos. 23-26.

A bi-monthly selection of publications and articles on housing and planning received in the Department of Housing and Urban Development Library. Publications are listed by subjects and then authors with entry numbers. Includes geographic indexes and author indexes in each issue but no cumulative indexes are provided. This would be a much more valuable reference tool with the addition of cumulative indexes.

377. U.S. Department of Housing and Urban Development. **Periodicals Received in the Housing and Urban Development Department Library, Subject Index.** Washington, GPO, 1969. 49 p. Issuing Agency. LC Card No. 74-600762. HH 1.28:76

This is a handy selection tool for periodicals in the fields of housing and urban development. Periodicals are listed in two sections, first alphabetically by titles and second by subject. Includes no information about the periodicals.

378. U.S. Department of Housing and Urban Development. Renewal Assistance Administration. **Urban Renewal Directory: June 30, 1969.** Washington, GPO, 1969. 137 p. Issuing Agency. LC Card No. 68-61152. HH 7.8/2:969

This directory is issued every six months and covers local urban renewal programs approved for federal assistance under Title I of the Housing Act of 1949. These include Urban Renewal Projects, Neighborhood Development Programs, General Neighborhood Renewal Plans, Feasibility Surveys, Code Enforcement Projects, Demolition Projects, Community Renewal Programs and Demonstration Programs. Consists of two parts: Part A—Summary tables by program; Part B—listing of programs by region, state, locality. In tabular form, shows location, type ID number, approval dates and grant status.

379. U.S. Small Business Administration. **Real Estate Business.** By Karl G. Pearson. Washington, SBA, 1969. 11 p. (Small Business Bibliography, no. 65). Issuing Agency. SBA 1.3:65

One in a series of bibliographies prepared for persons with specific interests in certain aspects of small business.

PART TWO

SCIENCE & ENGINEERING

SCIENCE & ENGINEERING

GENERAL WORKS

380. U.S. National Science Foundation. **Annual Report.** Washington, GPO, 1968. 279 p. $1.25. LC Card No. 52-60336. NS 1.1:968

1968 edition contains valuable reference aids in the appendixes:

(1) "Directory of the National Science Board, Staff Committees, and Advisory Panels" lists personnel.

(2) "Patents Resulting from Activities Supported by the National Science Foundation"—by patent number.

(3) "National Science Foundation—Supported Scientific Conferences, Symposia, and Advanced Science Seminars"—by type of conference, with address, and dates.

(4) "Publications of the National Science Foundation."

BIBLIOGRAPHIES

381. U.S. Atomic Energy Commission. **Science and Society Bibliography, 1965-67.** Prep. by the staff of the Atomic Energy Commission Library, with subject index by Hugh E. Voress. Springfield, Va., CFSTI, 1968. 87 p. $3.00. Y 3.At7:22/TID-3916

382. U.S. National Bureau of Standards. **National Bureau of Standards Films.** Washington, National Bureau of Standards, 1968. 32 p. Issuing Agency. C13.2:F48/968-2

Lists films available to scientific and professional organizations, colleges and universities, high schools and others for nonprofit, noncommercial showings. Films are listed under three headings: Science, weights and measures, and dental research and techniques. Gives title, data, physical description and a brief synopsis for each film.

383. U.S. National Bureau of Standards. **Publications of the National Bureau of Standards, 1966-67.** By Betty L. Oberholtzer. Washington, GPO, 1969. 213 p. $2.00. LC Card No. 48-47112. C 13.10:305

Includes National Bureau of Standards publications from July 1966 through December 1967 and publications of National Bureau of Standards staff members by private publishers for 1966 through 1967.

384. U.S. National Science Foundation. **Science Facilities Bibliography.** Washington, GPO, 1969. 47 p. $0.35. LC Card No. 79-602480. NS 1.13:F11/969

This bibliography is a list of articles and papers in the science facilities literature collection of the National Science Foundation's Architectural Services Staff. It was designed to "help persons searching for data on the design of science facilities." Arranged alphabetically by author under broad subject categories. An appendix lists publishers and distribution sources. Not indexed.

385. U.S. Naval Oceanographic Office. **Selected Readings in Marine Sciences, Fall 1969.** Comp. by Norman T. Edwards and Suzanne E. DeCarre. Washington, GPO, 1969. 32 p. $0.45. LC Card No. 79-604627. D 203.22/3:129

Designed for the general reader with an interest in marine sciences, this bibliography lists publications in the following areas: oceanography, marine biology, marine geology, diving, and government publications. Complete bibliographical citations including interest levels (juvenile, adult, technical) are given. Not annotated or indexed.

DIRECTORIES

386. U.S. National Bureau of Standards. **Calibration and Test Services of the National Bureau of Standards.** H. L. Mason, ed. Washington, GPO, 1968. 200 p. $1.75. LC Card No. 63-60099. C 13.10:250/968

"This publication contains a descriptive listing, item by item, of most of the test and calibration work done at the National Bureau of Standards with the respective fees." Divided into seven sections: General; Electricity, Washington Services; Optical and Dimensional Metrology; Mechanics; Heat; Radiation Physics; and Electricity, Boulder Services. An eighth section is the schedule of fees for measurement services. The entire work is "fully indexed providing easy access to data on specific measurement services." Includes information about the Bureau's organization, procedures for requesting tests, and the reports issued on such tests. The 1968 edition supersedes the 1965 edition and all its supplements.

387. U.S. National Science Foundation. **Guide to Programs.** Rev. ed. Washington, GPO, 1969. 78 p. $0.75. NS 1.20:P94/969

Designed to provide summary information about all support programs of the National Science Foundation. Each program listed gives the basic purposes, requirements, closing dates, and other information for making application. Divided into seven parts: research, education, institutional science, combined programs, international science, science information, and science planning and policy.

388. U.S. National Science Foundation. **Scientific and Technical Personnel in the Federal Government, 1967.** Prep. by Joel L. Barnes. Washington, GPO, 1969. 40 p. $0.50. LC Card No. 63-60142. NS 1.22:G74/967

Presents information about the scientific and technical personnel employed by the federal government, their occupations, employment by agencies, salaries, and detailed information on their work activities.

PATENTS

389. U.S. Patent Office. **General Information Concerning Patents.** Washington, GPO, 1969. 40 p. $0.30. C 21.2:P27/969

Presents a brief introduction to patent matters including: the workings of the Patent Office, what applicants must do and definitions of patents, copyrights and trademarks.

390. U.S. Patent Office. **Index of Patents Issued from the Patent Office, 1968.** Washington, GPO, 1969. 2 pts. (Pt. 1, 1406 p., $11.50, and pt. 2, 299 p., $4.50). LC Card No. 30-26211. C 21.5/2:968/pts.1&2

Part I: **List of Patentees,** an alphabetical list of persons or companies having new or reissued patents. Also includes lists of design patentees, plant patentees, disclaimers and dedications, and decisions published in the 1968 **Official Gazette.** Gives patent number for each patentee.

Part II: **Index of Subjects of Inventions,** is arranged by class and subclass number in accordance with Patent Office classification, with patent numbers following these classes. There is a list of class titles in class number order and an alphabetical list of class titles which must be consulted in order to find patents of a particular subject. Includes supplementary lists of libraries receiving issues of the U.S. Patents, of libraries receiving the **Official Gazette,** and a summary of the number of patents issued annually from 1836 to 1968.

391. U.S. Patent Office. **Index of Trademarks Issued from the Patent Office, 1968.** Washington, GPO, 1969. 323 p. $4.25. LC Card No. 30-26199. C 21.5/3:968

"Includes the registrants of all trademark registrations issued during the year; and also registrants of trademarks published in the **Official Gazette** . . ., and registrants of trademark registrations renewed, canceled, surrendered, amended, disclaimed, corrected, etc. during the year . . ." Arranged alphabetically by name of registrant with address and registration information.

AGRICULTURAL SCIENCES
GENERAL WORKS

392. U.S. National Agricultural Library. **Drainage of Agricultural Land; an Annotated Bibliography of Selected References, 1956-64.** Washington, National Agricultural Library, 1968. 524 p. (Library List No. 91.) Issuing Agency. LC Card No. Agr68-287. A 17.17:91

This bibliography was compiled to "keep up with the demand for information on both surface and subsurface drainage." Arranged alphabetically under broad subjects with some annotations. Author and subject indexes.

BIBLIOGRAPHIES

393. U.S. National Agricultural Library. **Available Bibliographies and Lists.** Rev. ed. Washington, National Agricultural Library, 1968. 2 p. (Library List No. 25.) Free. LC Card No. Agr46-109. A 17.17:25/13

The 1968 edition is the 13th revision of this bibliography. Lists bibliographies and "library lists" available from the National Agricultural Library.

394. U.S. National Agricultural Library. **Linneana in the Collection of the National Agricultural Library.** Comp. by Mortimer L. Naftalin. Washington, National Agricultural Library, 1968. 43 p. (Library List No. 89.) Issuing Agency. LC Card No. Agr68-197. A 17.17:89

This is the second in a series of bibliographies on the historical books in the National Agricultural Library. It lists monographs which were written by or about the botanist Carl von Linne. Citations are arranged chronologically and date from 1735 to 1968 including a physical description of the book and National Agricultural Library call number. Indexed by authors and subjects.

395. U.S. National Agricultural Library. **Serial Publications Indexed in the Bibliography of Agriculture.** Rev. ed. Washington, National Agricultural Library, 1968. 94 p. (Library List No. 75.) Issuing Agency. LC Card No. Agr63-209. A 17.17:75/4

An alphabetical listing of the periodicals indexed in the **Bibliography of Agriculture** which has now ceased publication.

DICTIONARIES

396. U.S. Department of Agriculture. **Glossary of Terms Used in ASCS and Related Programs; Production Adjustment, Price Support, Commodity Operations, Export Activities, Conservation and Land Use.** Washington, GPO, 1969. 150 p. Issuing Agency. LC Card No. 72-604731. A 1.76:371

"The purpose of this glossary is to familiarize the reader with terminology used in programs administered by the Agricultural Stabilization and Conservation Service, and other selected Departmental operations that touch on ASCS programs." Includes those terms that are in use currently. Listed with the terms are project names (e.g. Agricultural Conservation Program) and descriptions.

DIRECTORIES

397. U.S. Agricultural Research Service. **Directory of Agricultural Research Service.** Washington, GPO, 1968. 101 p. $0.25. LC Card No. Agr68-96. A 1.89/3:968

Lists ARS offices and key personnel in Washington, the states, and foreign countries. Index of agricultural specialists refers to the office in which each is located.

398. U.S. Consumer and Marketing Service. Grain Division. **Grain Inspection Points.** Hyattsville, Md., Grain Division, 1968. 56 p. Issuing Agency. A 88.2:G76/6/968

"Shows the places in the United States where grain inspection services are provided under the authority of the U.S. Grain Standards Act." The purpose of the publication is to enable "interested persons . . . to know where they may have their grain inspected to determine the quality, to determine the best routings to obtain inspections, and to arrange inspections in compliance with the inspection requirements of the Act." Part I, "Established Inspection Points," shows places where grain inspection services are regularly provided. Part 2, "Designated Inspection Points," lists places where grain inspection services are available on request. Both are arranged by state and city.

INDEXES

399. U.S. Agricultural Research Service. **Annotated Index of Registered Fungicides and Nematicides, Their Uses in the United States.** By Edward P. Carter, Daniel O. Betz and Charles T. Mitchell. Washington, GPO, 1969. 1392 p. $9.00. LC Card No. 73-604359. A 77.302:F96

The purpose of this publication is to "give those persons responsible for providing recommendations for the use of fungicides and nematicides information relating to active ingredients, formulations and patterns of use that have been accepted for Federal registration, and for which labels bearing adequate directions and cautions for the protection of the public are available in channels of trade." The first two sections list the fungicides and nematicides and gives the ingredients, methods of application, uses and maximum dosage allowable. The appendix lists quantities of water required for full fungicide coverage for a variety of plants, and contains a guide to recommended distances between rows of plants. Chemical and use indexes refer to the code numbers assigned each fungicide and nematicide in the first two parts.

STATISTICS

400. U.S. Department of Agriculture. **Agricultural Statistics 1969.** Washington, GPO, 1969. 631 p. $2.75. A 1.47:969

An annual statistical source on agricultural production, supplies, consumption, facilities, costs and returns. Includes historical series which are generally limited to data beginning with 1954/55 or the most recent 10 years. Contains 14 tables on such things as livestock, products, farm resources, income and expenses, support programs, taxes, insurance and credit, etc. Also contains a list of conversion factors and an index.

401. U.S. Department of Agriculture. **Handbook of Agricultural Charts, 1969.** Washington, GPO, 1969. 146 p. $0.65. LC Card No. 64-62697. A 1.76:373

Contains many charts and graphs which are available from the Department of Agriculture as photographic prints or slides. The charts cover such topics as the domestic agricultural situation, foreign production and trade, population and rural development, and commodity trends. A handy reference source for general agricultural information.

ANIMAL HUSBANDRY

402. U.S. Agricultural Research Service. **DHIA Sire Summary List.** Washington, Agricultural Research Service, 1969. 445 p. Issuing Agency. A 77.15: 44-211

This publication is the Agricultural Research Service record of bulls. It explains the compilation of the sire summary and lists name, birth date, registration of sire, number for dam of bull and where bull is located. Appendix of artificial breeding organizations in the U.S. with addresses.

FORESTRY

403. U.S. Forest Service. **Forest Service Films Available on Loan for Educational Purposes to Schools, Civic Groups, Churches and Television.** Washington, GPO, 1969. 34 p. Issuing Agency. LC Card No. Agr52-366. A 13.55:969

Lists and describes films available from the Forest Service for loan and some for sale. Indexed by title.

404. U.S. Forest Service. **Forest Service Organizational Directory.** Washington, GPO, 1969. 142 p. $0.60. A 13.36/2:Or3/2

Shows the organization of the Forest Service with the addresses and telephone numbers of the main field offices and units. Lists personnel responsible for the various units, key functions, lines of work and research projects.

HOME ECONOMICS

405. U.S. Department of Agriculture. **Family Food Buying: A Guide for Calculating Amounts to Buy and Comparing Costs.** Washington, GPO, 1969. 60 p. $0.35. A 1.87:37

A helpful reference source for the housewife. This food buying guide can help purchasers decide how much food to buy for the number of servings needed and compare the costs of foods in various package sizes and forms.

406. U.S. Department of Agriculture. **Food for Us All: The Yearbook of Agriculture, 1969.** Washington, GPO, 1969. 360 p. Illus. $3.50. LC Card No. 76-604428. A 1.10:969

This Yearbook is designed as a "popular encyclopedia of food for the consumer." The first section describes the economics of food, the second covers buying and cooking food, and the third is devoted to nutrition and planning meals. Indexed.

HORTICULTURE

407. U.S. Agency for International Development. **Handbook of Tropical and Subtropical Horticulture.** Ed. by Ernest Mortensen and Ervin T. Bullard. Rev. ed. Washington, GPO, 1969. 186 p. Illus. $2.25. LC Card No. 73-604190. S 18.8:H78/969

Designed to meet the needs of AID, Peace Corps and other U.S. personnel involved in foreign assistance programs and to "fill the need for consolidated information in ready reference form" for the non-specialist. Arranged under broad headings such as Fruit and Tree Crops, Vegetable Crops, Insect Control on Vegetables, and Equipment Supplies and Materials. Names and addresses of sources of plant material, vegetable seed sources, equipment materials and supplies. Has a handy section on conversion factors, and a bibliography of general reference sources.

408. U.S. National Agricultural Library. **Historic Books and Manuscripts Concerning Horticulture and Forestry in the Collection of the National Agricultural Library.** Comp. by Mortimer L. Naftalin. Washington, National Agricultural Library, 1968. 106 p. (Library List No. 90.) Issuing Agency. LC Card No. Agr68-195. A 17.17:90

This is the third in a series which includes **Historical Books and Manuscripts Concerning General Agriculture in the Collection of the National Agricultural Library,** 1967 (Library List No. 86), and **Linneana in the Collection of the National Agricultural Library,** 1968 (Library List No. 89).

Titles published prior to 1800 (for European imprints) and 1830 (American imprints) are included, with a few selected works published at later dates. Gives full bibliographical information and includes National Agricultural Library call number, collation, and Library of Congress card number. Horticulture books are listed first, alphabetically by author, followed by those on forestry.

409. U.S. National Agricultural Library. **Sunflower; A Literature Survey, January 1960-June 1967.** Comp. by Merne H. Posey. Washington, National Agricultural Library, 1969. 133 p. (Library List No. 95). Issuing Agency. LC Card No. 70-603089. A 17.17:95

Intended as a general survey with no attempt at selectivity, this bibliography includes references to material on various aspects of sunflower cultivation and growth in the United States and abroad. Contains listings of books and articles on the growth and uses of the sunflower and on the production of sunflower oil and its by-products. Arranged alphabetically by author with very brief annotations. Indexed by authors (including joint authors) and subjects.

WILDLIFE MANAGEMENT

410. U.S. Bureau of Commercial Fisheries. **Fishery Publications Index, 1955-64: Publications of the Fish and Wildlife Service by Series, Authors and Subjects.** Comp. by George Washington University. Washington, GPO, 1969. 240 p. $1.75. LC Card No. 76-603664. I 49.4:296

This index is a serial list of the numbers issued in each publication series of the Fish and Wildlife Service. Although not annotated, full contents of each publication are listed when several different reports are issued in one volume. Author and subject indexes.

411. U.S. Bureau of Sport Fisheries and Wildlife. **Bureau of Sport Fisheries and Wildlife Publications in the Calendar Year 1967.** Prep. by Barbara A. Alexander. Washington, Bureau of Sport Fisheries and Wildlife, 1968. 11 p. Issuing Agency. LC Card No. 68-62318. I 49.18/6:967

Arranged by type of publications (e.g. refuge leaflets, regulatory announcements). Not annotated or indexed.

412. U.S. Department of the Interior. Library. **Index to Federal Aid Publications in Sport Fish and Wildlife Restoration and Selected Cooperative Research Project Reports.** Washington, Department of the Interior, 1968. 726 p. Issuing Agency. LC Card No. 68-62958. I 22.9:F52

The cooperative fish and wildlife reference indexing project was initiated in "direct response to the expressed needs of the Federal and State conservation administrators . . . The Federal Aid Division of the Bureau of Sport Fisheries and Wildlife is funding and supervising the project in association with the Departmental Library and the Denver Public Library." The purpose of the project is to provide "ready access to the wealth of information contained in the unpublished reports and the publications of the Dingell-Johnson and the Pittman-Robertson programs, as the Federal Aid work in sport fishery and wildlife conservation is popularly known." The proliferation of data necessitated the development of automated reference sources. The Interior Departmental library is responsible for processing the publications; the Denver Public Library, the unpublished reports. This index cites published material only ("similar listings will be made available by the Denver Public Library for unpublished reports") and includes all available from the beginning of the Federal Aid programs in the early 1940's through March 1968. The citations are by item numbers under broad subject headings with complete bibliographic data, source, state-federal aid number, list of descriptors, geographic index and LC Classification number for each. Includes both English and Latin descriptor indexes, an author index (with corporate authors listed separately at the end), and a geographic index.

413. U.S. Forest Service. **Range and Wildlife Habitat Publications Issued in 1967 by Forest Service Research Personnel and Cooperators.** Washington, Forest Service, 1968. 10 p. Issuing Agency. A 13.11/2:R16/3/967

Lists 91 publications on range and wildlife habitat research sponsored by the USDA Forest Service in 1967. Not annotated or indexed.

ASTRONOMY

GENERAL WORKS

414. U.S. Department of the Air Force. **UFOs and Related Subjects, an Annotated Bibliography.** By Lynn E. Catoe. Prep. by the Library of Congress Science and Technology Division. Washington, GPO, 1969. 401 p. Illus. $3.50. LC Card No. 68-62196. D 301.45/19-2:68-1656

"Believed to be the most comprehensive bibliography published" on this subject. Includes books, journal articles, pamphlets, conference proceedings, tapes, original manuscripts of "scholarly intent" in order to make "the bibliography as useful as possible for both scholars and general readers." More than 1600 citations are listed under broad subject headings with annotations ranging in length from one line to several paragraphs. The wide range of fields covered include the physical sciences, the occult sciences and selected fiction. A separate section contains a selection of recent cartoons on the subject. Author index.

NAVIGATION

415. U.S. Naval Observatory. **The Air Almanac, 1970, January-April.** Washington, GPO, 1969. 242 + A82 p. $3.75. D 213.7:970/1

This issue of the almanac provides the astronomical data required for air navigation covering the period from January to April, 1970.

416. U.S. Naval Observatory. **The American Ephemeris and National Almanac, 1971.** Washington, GPO, 1969. 520 p. $6.25. LC Card No. 7-35404. D 213.8:971

This Almanac, printed separately in Washington and London, provides in convenient form the data required for the practice of astronomical navigation at sea. The main contents of the Almanac consist of data from which the Greenwich Hour Angle and the declination of all the bodies used for navigation can be obtained for an instant of Greenwich Mean Time. There are also sections on times of rising and setting of sun and moon, and times of twilight, miscellaneous calendarial and planning data and auxiliary tables, including a list of Standard Times.

417. U.S. Naval Oceanographic Office. **Navigation Dictionary.** 2nd ed. Washington, GPO, 1969. 292 p. $3.00. LC Card No. 71-603652. D 203.22:220/969

A "comprehensive, authoritative and current dictionary of navigational terms" designed to serve the needs of "the navigator of any type of craft." Terms in fields related to navigation (e.g. astronomy, meteorology, cartography) are included but defined in the language and from the viewpoint of the navigator. Definitions are clearly understandable for the intelligent, interested layman, and include cross references to related terms. Includes separate sections for abbreviations, symbols and a brief bibliography.

BIOLOGICAL SCIENCES

ENTOMOLOGY

418. U.S. National Museum. **Bibliography and Index to the Scientific Contributions of Carl J. Drake for the Years 1914-67.** By Florence A. Ruhoff. Washington, GPO, 1968. 81 p. $0.45. LC Card No. 68-60954. SI 3.3:267

A complete bibliography of the works of Carl J. Drake, entomologist. Arranged chronologically by date of publication. Includes an index by order, family, genus and species of the insects he studied.

ZOOLOGY

GENERAL WORKS

419. U.S. Bureau of Commercial Fisheries. **A List of Marine Mammals of the World.** By Dale W. Rice and Victor B. Scheffer. Washington, Bureau of Commercial Fisheries, 1968. 16 p. Issuing Agency. I 49.15/2:579

Lists and classifies living and recently extinct marine mammals of the world with information regarding size, habitat and first discovery. Includes a brief bibliography.

420. U.S. Public Health Service. **Pictorial Keys to Anthropods, Reptiles, Birds and Mammals of Public Health Significance.** Washington, GPO, 1969. 192 p. Illus. $2.25. FS 2.60/7:Ar7/2

These 30 pictorial keys were devised by the U.S. Public Health Service to teach animal identification to people not specially trained in taxonomy. Covers centipedes, scorpions, ants, earwigs, termites, bats and other animals of public health significance. Drawings and diagrams are in black and white and vary in format. Schools and libraries, as well as public health trainees, should find these keys useful references.

BIBLIOGRAPHIES

421. U.S. Bureau of Commercial Fisheries. **Books and Articles on Marine Mammals.** By Ethel I. Todd. Washington, Bureau of Commercial Fisheries, 1968. 14 p. Issuing Agency. LC Card No. 70-601166. I 49.4:299

Emphasizing recent titles, this bibliography lists books and articles on identification, biology and commercial use of seals, sea lions, walrus, whales and dolphins. Includes both technical and popular items. Not annotated or indexed.

422. U.S. Bureau of Sport Fisheries and Wildlife. **Some Publications on Fish Culture and Related Subjects.** Washington, Bureau of Sport Fisheries and Wildlife, 1968. 16 p. Issuing Agency. I 49.28:448/4

Publications listed under general subjects. Not annotated or indexed.

CHEMISTRY

423. U.S. Bureau of Mines. **Helium: Bibliography of Technical and Scientific Literature, 1962; Including Papers on Alpha-Particles.** By Philip C. Tully and Lowell Stroud. Washington, GPO, 1969. 357 p. $3.25. I 28.27:8398

The first bibliography in this series, Bulletin 484 (1952), covered the literature from the discovery of helium in 1868 to 1947; the second work, Circular 8373 (1962), covers 1947 to 1962, and the current volume continues the bibliography through 1962. Bibliographies covering material published annually since 1962 are now being compiled. Contains 2072 citations to technical and scientific literature and alpha-particles abstracted by 12 abstract service publications during 1962. Citations are listed by 16 major subject classifications with many subheadings. Automatic data processing was used in compiling this bibliography. Includes subject and author index.

424. U.S. Department of the Interior. Office of Saline Water. **Desalting Plants Inventory Report, No. 1.** Compiled by Milton Sachs. Washington, GPO, 1968. 25 p. $0.35. I 1.87/4.1

"Inventory of world-wide land based desalting plants in operation and under construction capable of producing 25,000 gallons or more of fresh water daily." Includes historical and current statistics with projections of future developments. Includes plants arranged by country showing locations, number of units, capacity, year of installation and type of process.

DATA PROCESSING

425. U.S. Department of Commerce. **Computers, Selected Bibliographic Citations Announced in U.S. Government Research and Development Reports, 1966.** Washington, Department of Commerce, 1968. 86 p. Issuing Agency. C 1.54:C73

Accumulations of 1966 citations in **U.S. Government Research and Development Reports** on the subject of computers. Entries are arranged by accession numbers. Detailed annotations. No index.

426. U.S. Federal Council for Science and Technology. Committee on Scientific and Technical Information. Panel on Operation Techniques and Systems. **Selected Mechanized Scientific and Technical Information Systems.** Ed. by Lynn Ockerman, Anna E. Cacciapaglia, and Melvin Weinstock. Prep. by Herner and Company. Washington, GPO, 1968. 143 p. $1.50. LC Card No. 68-61231. Y 3.F31/16:2M46

The purpose of this directory is "to describe 13 computer-based operational systems designed primarily for the announcement, storage, retrieval and secondary distribution of scientific and technical reports." For each system, this lists managers, functions, subject coverage, input processes, indexing services, personnel of various types, equipment, organizational affiliation with other systems, method of evaluation, and persons to contact for further information. Includes a list of acronyms, personal index and subject index.

427. U.S. General Services Administration. Federal Supply Service. **Inventory of Automatic Data Processing Equipment in the United States Government.** Washington, GPO, 1968. 241 p. $1.75. GS 2.15:968

Published "to provide information on the number of electronic computers in use throughout the U.S. Government, including owned and leased, average monthly hours in service, operating and capital costs, and number of man-years devoted to ADP functions." Inventories computers by agencies which use them in one section, lists them by manufacturer in another.

428. U.S. National Bureau of Standards. Institute for Applied Technology. **Information Systems Handbook.** Comp. by L.C. Richardson. Springfield, Va., CFSTI, 1968. 78 p. $3.00. AD 673 499

Originally distributed at the 1968 conference of the Interagency Data Exchange Program, this proved so useful it was published for public use. "Compiled from data collected through an extensive survey on information centers." Groups data systems by the type of data provided in the first section. Main directory is a detailed listing of the systems. For each it lists name of system, reference (where applicable), sponsor, type of system, subject coverage, and person to contact. Includes a bibliography of reference tools on the subject. No index.

ENVIRONMENTAL SCIENCE

GENERAL WORKS

429. U.S. Congress. Atomic Energy Joint Committee. **Selected Materials on Environmental Effects of Producing Electric Power, August 1969.** Washington, GPO, 1969. 563 p. $2.50. LC Card No. 78-604048. Y 4.At7/1:E12/2

430. U.S. Department of Defense. **Glossary of Environmental Terms (Terrestrial).** 2nd Printing. Washington, GPO, 1968. 149 p. Issuing Agency. D 7.10: 1165/2nd Print.

The purpose of this glossary is "to facilitate the exchange of information within the broad field of environmental engineering, by providing a common vocabulary for use in this field." It is intended primarily for use by engineers, technicians, contractors and administrators who are involved in "developmental and testing activities involving any aspect of the terrestrial environment but who are not specialists in the sciences that treat these subjects." Its scope is limited to terms which refer to "environments on the land surfaces of the earth and adjacent portions of the oceans and lower atmosphere that have a direct effect on surface conditions. Definitions are technical and contain source symbols explained in the back of the volume.

Related publications include **Air Force Glossary of Standardized Terms and Definitions** and NASA's **Dictionary of Technical Terms for Aerospace Use** for terms describing upper atmospheric and space environments, **Glossary of Oceanographic Terms** for marine environments and **Glossary of Meteorology** for terms describing atmospheric phenomena.

AIR POLLUTION

431. U.S. Public Health Service. **Air Pollution Publications, A Selected Bibliography with Abstracts, 1966-1968.** Comp. by the Science and Technology Division, Library of Congress for the National Air Pollution Control Administration. Washington, GPO, 1969. 522 p. (Public Health Service Publication No. 979). $4.50. LC Card No. 63-60159. FS 2.24:A71/966-68

Contains 1000 entries for the period 1966-68. PHS Publications No. 979 (rev. 1966) covers 1963-66 and Publications No. 979 (rev. 1964) covers 1955-63. Consists of references, with abstracts, to journal articles, books, conference papers and some report literature originating with the National Air Pollution Control Administration Staff and grantees. Arranged in 12 broad subject categories such as emission sources, measurement, and legal aspects. Author and subject indexes. Addendum of articles which appeared in the last quarter of 1968.

432. U.S. Public Health Service. Consumer Protection and Environmental Health Service. **Air Quality Data from the National Air Sampling Networks and Contributing State and Local Networks.** Washington, GPO, 1968. 157 p. Issuing Agency. FS 2.307:68-9

"Summarizes data on particulate and gaseous pollutants gathered during 1966 at the cooperating stations." Includes 180 stations arranged first by state, then county and city. Measures chemical pollutants in micrograms per cubic meter with measurements divided by quarterly periods.

433. U.S. Public Health Service. Division of Air Pollution. **Air Pollution and the Kraft Pulping Industry; An Annotated Bibliography.** By Paul A. Kenline and Jeremy M. Hales. Washington, GPO, 1968. 122 p. Issuing Agency. FS 2.300:Ap-4

"Provides an annotated bibliography of articles concerning measurement and control of kraft mill airborne pollution currently available in the literature." Also includes a description of the kraft pulping process, a survey of mill emissions and a consideration of control measures. Annotations are detailed and technical. Includes some unpublished papers. Indexed.

434. U.S. Public Health Service. **Free Films on Air Pollution on Loan for Group Showing.** Washington, GPO, 1969. 23 p. Illus. $0.15. FS 2.2:Ai7/30/969

Includes descriptions of "professionally produced films that illustrate the serious problem of air pollution and what to do about it." Gives detailed synopses, physical descriptions, and addresses for every film. Notes those films cleared for television.

CONSERVATION

435. U.S. National Agricultural Library. **Beauty for America, January 1966-May 1968.** Comp. by Minnie L. Fuller. Washington, National Agricultural Library, 1968. 32 p. (Library List No. 94). Issuing Agency. LC Card No. Agr68-334. A 17.17:94

This is a bibliography of literature on landscape improvement, slum clearance, highway scenery enhancement and related areas of conservation for the period from 1966 through May 1968, including programs on the federal, state, municipal and personal levels. Arranged alphabetically by author with a word or phrase of annotation if the subject of the book isn't made apparent in the title. Author and subject indexes.

436. U.S. Soil Conservation Service. **Soil and Water Conservation Districts.** Hyattsville, Md., Soil Conservation Service, 1968. 72 p. $0.50. LC Card No. 50-61311. A 57.32:968

Lists 3000 soil and water conservation districts at random under the 50 states, Puerto Rico and the Virgin Islands. Provides approximate acreage, number of farms, and location for each district.

437. U.S. Tennessee Valley Authority. **Flood Damage Prevention; An Indexed Bibliography.** 6th ed. Knoxville, Tenn., TVA, 1969. 43 p. Issuing Agency. LC Card No. 74-604276. Y 3.T25:31F65/969

A bibliography of materials about flood damage prevention and flood plain regulation "with only selected items pertaining to flood control." Arranged alphabetically by author under year of publication, without annotations. Subject index.

WATER POLLUTION

438. U.S. Federal Water Pollution Control Administration. **Water and Water Pollution Control, Selected List of Publications.** Washington, Federal Water Pollution Control Administration, 1968. 15 p. Issuing Agency. I 67.14:W29

Includes publications which were selected "to increase the average reader's knowledge of an environmental problem which is assuming greater importance each year." Some entries are annotated. Includes addresses of FWPCA project offices, regional offices, and laboratories.

439. U.S. Federal Water Pollution Control Administration. **Water Pollution Control Research, Development, Demonstration, and Training Projects, 1968: Grants and Contract Awards, Research Grants, Research Contracts, Demonstration Grants, Storm and Combined Sewer Grants, Storm and Combined Sewer Contracts, Advanced Waste Treatment Grants, Advanced Waste Treatment Contracts, Individual Waste Treatment Grants, Individual Waste Treatment Contracts, and Training Grants Research Fellowships.** Washington, GPO, 1968. 140 p. Issuing Agency. LC Card No. 67-60435. I 67.13:968

"The purposes of these grants are to encourage, cooperate with, and assist appropriate agencies, institutions, and individuals in the conduct of the studies and training relating to the causes, control and prevention of water pollution." Divided into four sections: research grants; demonstration grants; training grants; and research fellowships. In each section, there are summaries of grants by states followed by complete lists of grants awarded. Tells location and investigator, project title and number, and amount of each grant.

EARTH SCIENCES

GEOLOGY

440. U.S. Geological Survey. **Bibliography of North American Geology, 1965.** Washington, GPO, 1969. 1144 p. $4.75. LC Card No. GS24-38. I 19.3:1235

This is a standard bibliography in the field of North American geology and is published annually with some cumulations. It is arranged alphabetically by authors. Cites journal articles, books, professional papers, and entries from

Dissertation Abstracts. Detailed subject and geographical index.

Cumulative editions are: Bulletin No. 746-47, 1785-1918; Bulletin No. 823, 1919-28; Bulletin No. 937, 1929-39; Bulletin No. 1049, 1940-49; Bulletin No. 1195, 1950-59.

441. U.S. Geological Survey. **Descriptive Catalog of Selected Aerial Photographs of Geologic Features in Areas Outside the United States.** By Charles R. Warren and others. Washington, GPO, 1969. 23 + 13 p. Illus. $1.25. LC Card No. GS68-290. I 19.16:591

The USGS selected 67 sets of aerial photographs that illustrate a variety of geologic features in Antarctica, South and Central America, the southwest Pacific, Iran, Japan, the Arabian Peninsula, Pakistan and mainland China. This is a catalog of samples of these sets which are available for purchase from the USGS. Lists, for each set, the location, scale of photography, and a brief description of the features. One sample photograph from each set is included in a separate section.

442. U.S. Geological Survey. **Descriptive Catalog of Selected Aerial Photographs of Geologic Features in the United States.** By Charles Denny and others. Washington, GPO, 1968. 55 p. $2.25. LC Card No. GS67-292. I 19.16:590

A valuable reference tool for anyone involved in geological work. Lists and describes 317 sets of photographs assembled by the USGS which "illustrate numerous types of geologic features in the U.S." Information includes the location, scale of the photograph, a brief description of the features illustrated, and a reference to a geologic report or topographic map of the area. One reduced photograph from each set is shown in a separate section at the back of the book. Indexed by geologic features. Includes a map showing the various regions and complete ordering information.

HYDROLOGY

443. U.S. Geological Survey. **Bibliography of Hydrology of the United States and Canada, 1964.** Comp. by J.R. Randolph, N.M. Baker and R.G. Deike. Washington, GPO, 1969. 232 p. $1.00. LC Card No. GS68-391. I 19.13:1864

"This volume lists references to books, journal articles and other publications in the field of hydrology published in the United States and Canada during 1964 and some references . . . from international journals in which American authors frequently publish." Entries are alphabetical by author with full bibliographical citations but no annotations. Indexed by subjects.

444. U.S. Water Resources Council. **Annotated Bibliography on Hydrology and Sedimentation, 1963-65; United States and Canada.** Washington, GPO, 1969. 527 p. $4.50. Y3.W29:9/9

A guide to the literature of hydrology and sedimentation published in the U.S. and Canada from 1963 through 1965. Arranged alphabetically by author with full bibliographic information and brief annotation. Detailed subject index.

METEOROLOGY

GENERAL WORKS

445. U.S. Department of the Air Force. **Selected Annotated Bibliography on Lightning.** By Alvin L. Smith, Jr. and Dennis L. Boyer. Springfield, Va., CFSTI, 1969. 43 p. $3.00. LC Card No. 77-605026. D 301.40/2:69-8 (AD-697 020)

446. U.S. Environmental Science Services Administration. **Bibliography of Weather and Architecture.** By John F. Griffiths and M. Joan Griffiths. Springfield, Va., CFSTI, 1969. 72 p. $3.00. C 52.15/2:EDSTM-9 (PB-184 969)

447. U.S. Environmental Science Services Administration. **Catalog of U.S. Government Meteorological Research and Test Facilities.** Washington, GPO, 1969. 123 p. Illus. Issuing Agency. LC Card No. 79-604450. C 52.2:M56/3

Prepared under the guidance of the Interdepartmental Committee for Applied Meteorological Research, this catalog provides descriptions of facilities for meteorological research and testing which are operated by various agencies of the federal government. Facilities are listed first by governmental department and then by their names. Information for each includes location, operator or agency, description of available facilities and services, work capacity, service charges (if any), addresses for further information. Includes photographs of many areas listed and a subject index.

CLIMATOLOGY

448. U.S. Department of the Navy. Naval Air Systems Command. **U.S. Navy Marine Climatic Atlas of the World: Volume 8, The World.** By H.L. Crutcher and O.M. Davis. Washington, GPO, 1969. 179 p. $9.00. LC Card No. Map56-29. D 202.2:At6/v.8

Other volumes in this series are:
1. North Atlantic Ocean, 1955
2. North Pacific Ocean, 1957
3. Indian Ocean, 1958
4. South Atlantic Ocean, 1958
5. South Pacific Ocean, 1959
6. Arctic Ocean, 1963
7. Antarctic Ocean, 1965

"This volume presents meteorological information for the surface and upper levels of the atmosphere over the oceans of the earth and adjacent land areas." It combines the salient features of the preceding seven volumes, which treat individually each of the major ocean basins, to provide a "coherent presentation of the global maritime climatic regimes." Its purpose is to "provide a source for those requiring an up-to-date qualitative knowledge of the climates of the oceans."

449. U.S. Environmental Science Services Administration. **Climates of the World.** Washington, GPO, 1969. 28 p. $0.35. LC Card No. 77-602801. C 52.2:C61/3

"The principal features of climates of all the continents are discussed briefly." Maps illustrate worldwide temperatures and precipitation and tables show monthly and annual temperatures and precipitation. Includes sections on temperature extremes and extremes of average annual precipitation.

450. U.S. Environmental Science Services Administration. **Climatic Atlas of the United States.** Washington, GPO, 1968. 80 p. Illus. $4.25. LC Card No. 68-146. C 52.2:C61/2

"The purpose of this atlas is to depict the climate of the United States in terms of the distribution and variation of constituent climatic elements." The climate maps present a series of analyses showing the national distribution of mean, normal and/or extreme temperatures, precipitation, wind, barometric pressure, relative humidity, dewpoint, sunshine, sky cover, heating degree days, solar radiation and evaporation.

451. U.S. Environmental Science Services Administration. **Selective Guide to Climatic Data Sources.** Washington, GPO, 1969. 90 p. $1.00. LC Card No. 71-602769. C 30.66/2:4.11/2

This publication is designed to be of assistance to "potential users of climatological data by informing them of the availability of such data in published and unpublished form." Gives a brief review of pertinent historical facts associated with each publication, a list of the climatological tables and charts included, sale price or subscription rate and address. Index of published data lists separate categories (e.g. barometric pressure, rainfall) by time periods.

452. U.S. Public Health Service. National Air Pollution Administration. **The Climate of Cities: A Survey of Recent Literature.** Washington, GPO, 1969. 48 p. $0.55. FS 2.93/3:59

A survey of the literature on city climatology with emphasis on that written since 1962. The meteorological aspects of urban climate which are most fully covered are temperature, humidity, visibility, radiation, wind and precipitation.

MINEROLOGY

453a. U.S. Bureau of Mines. **Minerals Yearbook, 1968: V. 1-2, Metals, Minerals and Fuels.** Prep. by the Staff of the Bureau of Mines. Washington, GPO, 1969. 1208 p. Illus. $6.25. LC Card No. 33-26551. I 28.37:968/v.1,2

453b. U.S. Bureau of Mines. **Minerals Yearbook, 1968: V. 3, Area Reports, Domestic.** Prep. by the Staff of the Bureau of Mines. Washington, GPO, 1969. 838 p. Illus. $5.00. LC Card No. 33-26551. I 28.37:968/v.3

These volumes contain a comprehensive review of U.S. mining and metallurgy for 1968. Includes reports and statistics on economic developments, mining techniques, and production and trade.

Also issued as House Doc. 22, 91st Cong., 1st Session.

454. U.S. Bureau of Mines. **Minerals Yearbook, 1967: Volume 4, Area Reports, International.** Prep. by the Staff of the Bureau of Mines. Washington, GPO, 1969. 1036 p. $5.75. LC Card No. 33-26551. I 28.37:967/v.4

This is the 86th year of publication of this annual report of the U.S. mineral industry. Volume 4 was not published in 1966 and has now been reinstated. Contains 85 chapters presenting the latest available mineral statistics for more than 130 foreign countries and areas, and discusses the importance of minerals to the economies of these nations. A separate chapter reviews minerals in the world economy. Also issued as House Document 22, pt. 4, 91st Cong., 2nd Session.

NATURAL RESOURCES

455. U.S. Department of the Interior. **Natural Resources in Foreign Countries, A Contribution toward a Bibliography of Bibliographies.** Comp. by Mary Anglemyer. Washington, Department of the Interior, 1968. 113 p. Issuing Agency. LC Card No. 68-67278. I 22.9/1:9

Because "there is no national bibliography on natural resources and no comprehensive bibliography of area studies" and because of the need for such a bibliography, this work was initiated. It is "a preliminary listing and describes only a few of the existing bibliographies." Includes only those bibliographies which are arranged either by subject or geographically or in a "form which readily reveals this information." Includes only titles in English and western European languages in the libraries of the U.S. Department of the Interior, U.S. Department of State, U.S. Geological Survey, and the Joint Library of the International Monetary Fund and International Bank for Reconstruction and Development.

Lists general bibliographies first, followed by bibliographies on specific regions or states. Arranged alphabetically by author within each group. Some annotations. Author index.

456. U.S. Department of the Interior. **Permuted Title Index to Water Research Journals, 1967.** Washington, Department of the Interior, 1968. 396 p. Issuing Agency. LC Card No. 70-600544. I 1.2:W29/6/967

The purpose of this publication is to "supplement ongoing information services in the water resources field and to afford wider availability of useful bibliographical publications to scientists, engineers and others having water-related program responsibilities." The permuted title index lists a title under each significant word with an identification number. The identification number index then gives the author of the article along with the full citation. This publication is also available under the University of Cornell imprint.

457. U.S. Department of the Interior. **Water Resources Research Catalog, volume 4.** Washington, GPO, 1969. 1311 p. $8.50. I 2.94:4

This series presents "summary descriptions of current research on water resources problems," and makes available information on what is being done, by whom and where. This volume describes 4,501 active research projects and lists

5,749 investigators and 1,100 organizations. Describes both federally and privately supported projects. Indexed by subjects, investigators, contractors and supporting agencies.

458. U.S. Tennessee Valley Authority. **Indexed Bibliography of the Tennessee Valley Authority, Cumulative Supplement, January 1965-December 1966.** Knoxville, Tenn., Tennessee Valley Authority, 1968. 74 p. Issuing Agency. Y 3.T25: 31T25/2/965-66

Lists journal articles about the TVA program in numerical order. Entries are not annotated. Complete author and subject indexes.

OCEANOGRAPHY

459. U.S. Coast and Geodetic Survey. **Tidal Current Tables, Pacific Coast of North America and Asia.** Washington, GPO, 1969. 154 p. $2.00. LC Card No. 22-26900. C 4.23:970

Includes publications relating to tides and currents.

460. U.S. Coast and Geodetic Survey. **Tide Tables, High and Low Water Predictions, Central and Western Pacific Ocean and Indian Ocean, 1970.** Washington, GPO, 1969. 386 p. $2.00. LC Card No. 7-35369. C 4.15/6:970

Includes publications relating to tides and currents and an index map of tide table coverage.

461. U.S. Naval Oceanographic Office. **Films on Oceanography.** By R. P. Cuzon du Rest. Washington, GPO, 1969. 99 p. Illus. $1.00. D 203.24:C-4/3

Lists films under the following headings: (1) general oceanography; (2) biology; (3) chemistry; (4) engineering; (5) geology; and (6) physics. For each film listed the title, a brief synopsis, physical features, type of audience, source and price are listed. Indexed by titles.

SEISMOLOGY

462a. U.S. Coast and Geodetic Survey. **United States Earthquakes, 1936-40.** Washington, GPO, 1969. 332 p. Illus. $2.25. C 4.25/2:936-40

462b. U.S. Coast and Geodetic Survey. **United States Earthquakes, 1941-45.** Washington, GPO, 1969. 285 p. Illus. $3.00. LC Card No. 79-605005. C 4.25/2:941-45

Two compilations and reprints of annual issues of **United States Earthquakes.** This series also includes a compilation for 1928-35. Contains detailed technical information for each earthquake registered in the United States and regions under its jurisdiction during the years covered. Includes samples of seismograph and tilt-graph readings and photographs.

463. U.S. Coast and Geodetic Survey. **United States Earthquakes, 1967.** By Carl A. Von Hake and William K. Cloud. Ed. by Jerry L. Coffman. Washington,

GPO, 1969. 90 p. Illus. $1.25. LC Card No. 30-27161. C 4.25/2:967

This is the 1967 edition of the **Earthquakes** series, containing the same kind of information as above.

ENGINEERING

GENERAL WORKS

464. U.S. Bureau of Mines. **Bibliography of Investment and Operating Costs for Chemical and Petroleum Plants, January-December, 1968.** By Sidney Katell and William C. Morel. Washington, GPO, 1969. 132 p. $1.25. I 28.27:8415

This bibliography contains abstracts of articles concerned with all phases of cost engineering of chemical and petroleum plants from 15 journals. Indexed by subject and author.

465. U.S. Department of Defense. **Directory in Plastics: Knowledgeable Government Personnel.** By Norman E. Beach. Rev. ed. Springfield, Va., CFSTI, 1969. 126 p. $6.00. LC Card No. 67-60430. D 4.11:5C

The purpose of this directory is "to provide a means for the rapid identification and contacting of those personnel within the Department of Defense who are knowledgeable in all the various areas of plastics development, manufacture and use." Includes some personnel from other U.S. departments. Arranged first by department and division, then by subject, with name of specialists, division and telephone number. Includes a name index.

AERONAUTICAL & SPACE ENGINEERING

466. U.S. National Aeronautics and Space Administration. **Aerospace Bibliography.** Comp. by National Aerospace Education Council. 4th ed. Washington, GPO, 1968. 63 p. $0.40. LC Card No. 66-61596. NAS 1.19:48

A selective bibliography for the use of laymen, specifically "elementary and secondary school teachers, their pupils, and . . . the general adult reader." This is an "annotated and graded list of books, reference works, periodicals, and teaching aids dealing with space flight subjects." Reading level of each item is designated by code letters; a separate section lists teaching aids by subject with addresses needed to obtain them. Books are also listed by subjects with separate sections for reference materials and periodicals.

ELECTRICAL & ELECTRONIC ENGINEERING

467. U.S. Department of the Air Force. **Communications-Electronics Terminology.** Washington, GPO, 1968. 318 p. $2.00. D 301.7:100-39

Short Title: CED 3900

The purpose of this glossary is to "provide a comprehensive reference source of specialized terminology" in communication-electronics. Contains concise definitions of technical terms and a separate listing of abbreviations.

468. U.S. Public Health Service. **Regulations, Standards and Guides for Microwaves, Ultraviolet Radiation, and Radiation from Lasers and Television Receivers—**

An Annotated Bibliography. By Lloyd R. Setter and others. Washington, GPO, 1969. 77 p. Issuing Agency. LC Card No. 78-601117. FS 2.300:RH-35

An annotated bibliography of guidelines, standards and regulations pertaining to public health protection against electromagnetic radiation from television receivers, lasers, ultraviolet radiation and microwaves. Each category of radiation is treated in a separate section. Annotations include identification of the document, type of standard, limits and specifications, and general guidance.

MILITARY & NAVAL ENGINEERING

469. U.S. Department of the Air Force. Air University. Library. **Air University Library Index to Military Periodicals.** Ed. by V. Estelle Phillips. Washington, GPO, 1969. 4 issues. Issuing Agency. LC Card No. 51-4277. D 301.26/2:vol. no.

This index is available to libraries only. It is a subject index to periodical articles, including news items and editorials, from English language military and aeronautical periodicals which are not indexed in other standard periodical indexes.

470. U.S. Department of the Air Force. Air University. Library. **Art of War, Selected References.** Comp. by Mary Louise Pitts. Maxwell Air Force Base, Ala., Air University, 1968. 40 p. Issuing Agency. D 301.26/11:190(rev.)

An alphabetical listing of references to books and periodical articles on war arranged under the following subjects: principles of war, war in historical perspective, development of aerospace power, military geography, limited war, wars of national liberation, impact of war on society, arts, sciences and cultures, and rules of war. Not annotated or indexed.

471. U.S. Department of the Air Force. **Air Force Scientific Research Bibliography, volume 8, 1965.** By Thomas C. Goodwin and others. Washington, GPO, 1969. 939 p. $8.75. LC Card No. 61-60038. D 301.45/19-2:700/v.8

Part of a continuing series which contains "abstracts of all technical notes, technical reports, journal articles, books, symposium proceedings and monographs produced and published by scientists supported in whole or in part by the Air Force Office of Scientific Research."

472. U.S. Department of the Air Force. **Bibliography of AFCRL Publications from July 1, 1966 to September, 1967.** Springfield, CFSTI, 1968. 178 p. $3.00. D 301.45/42:73

Lists all of the Air Force Cambridge Research Laboratory in-house reports, journal articles and contractor reports issued from July 1, 1966 through September 30, 1967. A supplement to **Bibliography of AFCRL In-House Technical Reports** of March 1967. Planned to become a quarterly publication in the future.

473. U.S. Department of the Army. Office of the Chief of Military History. **Directory of U.S. Army Museums.** Washington, Department of the Army, 1969.

95 p. Issuing Agency. LC Card No. 71-601335. D 114.2:M97

The first edition of the official **Directory of U.S. Army Museums** lists 59 Army museums, 10 National Guard museums and 17 non-Army museums (National Park Service, Navy, Marine and others). Information was compiled from the results of a questionnaire survey. Part I lists and describes Army museums by Army areas, grouped by state. Part II lists all Army museum personnel alphabetically. Part III lists National Guard museums by state. Part IV consists of brief entries for certain important non-Army military museums. Part V lists organizations with an interest in history museums. Illustrated with a number of black and white photographs.

474. U.S. Department of the Army. **U.S. Army Directory of Technical Information Holdings and Services.** Alexandria, Va., Defense Documentation Center, 1969. 63 p. Issuing Agency. LC Card No. 77-602398. D 101.2:D62

This directory "identifies 111 Army sources of technical information that include 2200 specialized subject areas." Arranged by agency within the Army and indexed by subject matter and name. Gives description, lists subject specialties and size of document collection for each source.

NUCLEAR ENGINEERING

475. U.S. Atomic Energy Commission. Division of Technical Information. **Bibliographies of Atomic Energy Literature Issued or in Progress.** Springfield, Va., CFSTI, 1964- . Bimonthly. $3.00/copy. Y 3.At7:22/TID-3700+

The TID-3700 series is intended "to serve as a reference source to available current bibliographies and to announce those that are in progress, both domestic and foreign." References to bibliographies completed prior to 1966 are cumulated in TID-3043 (1958-1961) and TID-3350(1962-66). References to bibliographies completed since 1966 are listed in the TID-3700 series beginning with number 3739.

In three parts: "Bibliographies Issued," "Bibliographies in Preparation," and "Report Number Index," which includes availability of reports. Includes lists of national and international AEC depositories.

476. U.S. Atomic Energy Commission. Division of Technical Information. **Bibliographies of Interest to the Atomic Energy Program.** Comp. by Theodore F. Davis and others. Springfield, Va., CFSTI, 1968. $3.00. Y 3.At7:22/TID-3350

"References with abstracts are given for 2001 bibliographies and literature surveys compiled from 1962 through 1966 that are related to atomic energy. Entries are categorized by subject, and appropriate cross references are provided. A report number index showing availability is included together with a corporate author index."

Although arranged differently, this cumulates the supplements of TID-3043 (Rev. 2) to facilitate research.

477. U.S. Atomic Energy Commission. Division of Technical Information. **Corporate Author Headings Used by the U.S. Atomic Energy Commission in Cataloging Reports.** 9th rev. Springfield, Va., CFSTI, 1969. 172 p. $3.00. Y 3.At7:22/TID-5059(Rev. 969)

The authority list of corporate names used by the AEC; printed from a computer-maintained file. Includes "see" references from variant forms to accepted forms; "x" or "refer from" references under accepted forms with identifying numbers of variant forms, and "see also" references for name changes which direct to latest names.

478. U.S. Atomic Energy Commission. Division of Technical Information. **Subject Headings Used by the USAEC Division of Technical Information.** Ed. by Stanley F. Lanier. 9th rev. ed. Springfield, Va., CFSTI, 1969. 276 p. $3.00. Y 3.At7:22/TID-5001 (Rev. 969-2)

"The subject heading authority is an information indexing and retrieval tool used by the Division of Technical Information Extension in preparing subject indexes to the literature abstracted in **Nuclear Science Abstracts** and in searching these indexes either by manual or machine-assisted means."

Includes two appendixes: a list of elements and their symbols and a list of acceptable subheadings.

479. U.S. Atomic Energy Commission. Office of the Assistant General Manager for Reactors. **Nuclear Reactors Built, Being Built, or Planned in the United States as of January 30, 1968.** Springfield, Va., CFSTI, 1968. 34 p. $3.00. Y 3.At7:44N47/967

"This compilation contains unclassified information about facilities built, being built, or planned in the United States for domestic use or export as of June 30, 1968 which are capable of sustaining a nuclear chain reaction." Lists owners, locations, principal contractors, types and power statistics for each.

480. U.S. Atomic Energy Commission. **Reading Resources in Atomic Energy.** Oak Ridge, Tenn., Atomic Energy Commission, 1968. 20 p. Issuing Agency. LC Card No. 68-60542. Y 3.At7:54At7/3

Contains one list of atomic energy books for children and one for adults. Lists include selected basic readings on atomic energy and closely related subjects. Each list is alphabetical by titles. One author index to both lists. Includes a list of publishers' addresses.

481. U.S. Atomic Energy Commission. **Selected Annotated Bibliography of Civil, Industrial and Scientific Uses for Nuclear Explosives.** Comp. by Robert G. West and Robert C. Kelly. Springfield, Va., CFSTI, 1969. 43 p. $3.00. Y 3.At7:22/TID-3522(rev. 8, suppl. 1)

482. U.S. Atomic Energy Commission. **Technical Books and Monographs Sponsored by the Atomic Energy Commission.** 6th ed. Washington, Atomic

Energy Commission, 1968. 92 p. Issuing Agency. LC Card No. 62-60273.
Y 3.At7:44T22/968

The Atomic Energy Commission, "recognizing the needs of scientists, engineers, and others throughout the world for information presented in readily usable form, has sponsored the publication of technical books and monographs for the past 20 years." This lists more than 200 such AEC sponsored books published since 1947 and nearly 50 books and monographs in preparation. In two main sections: Published and In Preparation, with books listed and described under subject headings. Author and title indexes.

483. U.S. Library of Congress. **Nuclear Science in Mainland China; a Selected Bibliography.** By Chi Wang. Washington, GPO, 1968. 70 p. $0.70. LC Card No. 68-62146. LC 33.2:C44/4

This reference guide consists of "a selection of titles of research reports, studies, articles and other informative materials" for preliminary research on nuclear science in Mainland China. Part one lists items in Chinese with emphasis on works published between 1950 and 1966; Part two contains items in other languages, primarily English, from 1964 to 1967. Items are numbered and listed under broad subject headings. Brief annotations are provided for most entries. Indexed by authors and subjects. Includes a list of Chinese journals cited.

PUBLIC SAFETY ENGINEERING

CIVIL DEFENSE

484. U.S. Office of Civil Defense. **Fallout Shelters, Guide to Informative Literature.** Prep. by McGuaghan and Johnson, Architects. Washington, Office of Civil Defense, 1968. 15 p. Issuing Agency. D 119.13:45

Lists a number of OCD publications which describe fallout shelter programs and shelter design principles. Annotated. All publications listed are free from the Office of Civil Defense.

485. U.S. Office of Civil Defense. **Publications Index.** Washington, Office of Civil Defense, 1969. 38 p. Issuing Agency. LC Card No. 59-61734. D 119.11: 20/969

Lists publications in the "Federal Civil Defense Guide" series, technical publications, informational and educational publications, posters and displays, industrial civil defense publications and rural civil defense publications in separate sections. Includes instructions for ordering and a list of state civil defense officials.

486. U.S. Office of Civil Defense. Staff College. **Abbreviations and Definitions of Terms Commonly Used in Civil Defense.** Battle Creek, Mich., Office of Civil Defense, 1968. 23 p. Issuing Agency. D 119.11:51

For use primarily in OCD National Training Programs, to "assist in the understanding and standardization of many civil defense terms." Useful for anyone interested in this area. Dictionary section follows abbreviations list.

FIRE SCIENCES

487. U.S. Forest Service. **Fire, Summary of Literature in United States from the Mid-1920's to 1966.** By Charles T. Cushwa. Washington, Forest Service, 1968. 117 p. Issuing Agency. A 13.63/13-12:F51

"This summarizes literature concerning properties, uses, and effects of controlled and uncontrolled fire, from the mid-1920's to the present published mainly in the United States." Alphabetically by author with a complete subject index. Not annotated.

LAW ENFORCEMENT

488. U.S. Federal Aviation Administration. **Hijacking: Selected References.** Comp. by Ann O'Brien. Springfield, Va., CFSTI, 1969. 22 p. $3.00. LC Card No. 71-602813. TD 4.17/3:18

489. U.S. Office of Law Enforcement Assistance. **LEAA Grants and Contracts, Fiscal 1966-68.** Washington, GPO, 1968. 105 p. $1.00. J 1.33:966-68-2

"Under the Law Enforcement Assistance Act which began November 1, 1965 and ended June 19, 1968, Federal support was awarded to 359 separate projects." Lists and describes projects by type in each fiscal year. Index of grants by number and location. Includes a list of grants in numerical order.

MEDICAL SCIENCES

GENERAL WORKS

490. U.S. National Institutes of Health. **Medical and Health Related Sciences Thesaurus.** (2nd ed.) Washington, GPO, 1969. 460 p. Issuing Agency. LC Card No. 71-601859. FS 2.88:M46/969

"Compiled and maintained as an indexing authority list for the preparation of the annual Research Grants Index, a subject-matter index of research projects supported by the Public Health Service," this is also useful aid for research analysts, librarians and information specialists connected with medical information systems.

491. U.S. National Library of Medicine. **National Library of Medicine Classification.** Prep. by Emilie Wiggins. 3rd ed. Washington, GPO, 1969. 323 p. $2.75. LC Card No. 78-605331. HE 20.3602:C56/969

Presents the National Library of Medicine classification scheme for shelf list arrangement of books in the field of medicine and its related sciences as supplemented by the Library of Congress classification for subjects bordering on medicine and for general reference materials.

BIBLIOGRAPHIES

492. U.S. Children's Bureau. Clearinghouse for Research in Child Life. **Bibliography on the Battered Child.** Washington, GPO, 1969. 22 p. Issuing Agency. LC Card No. 76-605031. FS 17.212:B22

A listing of periodical articles, books, theses, dissertations and conference reports on the battered child. Includes a section on research studies reported to the Clearinghouse for Research in Child Life which includes abstracts of the studies.

493a. U.S. National Library of Medicine. **Film Reference Guide for Medicine and Allied Sciences.** By the Federal Advisory Council on Medical Training Aids. Washington, GPO, 1968. 386 p. $2.75. LC Card No. 56-60040. FS 2.211:968

493b. U.S. National Library of Medicine. **Film Reference Guide for Medicine and Allied Sciences.** 1969 **Supplement.** By the Federal Advisory Council on Medical Training Aids. Washington, GPO, I969. 74 p. $0.75.
    1968 edition provides a "basic catalog of selected audiovisuals used in biomedical education by member agencies" of the Federal Advisory Council on Medical Training Aids. "Each audiovisual included is currently available for loan or rental. No films are listed which are for sale only." Arranged by subject, with subject and title indexes, and a list of distributors. Includes a physical description of the film (i.e. time, sound, color or black and white, etc.)

494. U.S. Public Health Service. Division of Regional Medical Programs. **Selected Bibliography of Regional Medical Programs.** Washington, Public Health Service, 1968. 26 p. Issuing Agency. LC Card No. 68-67228. FS 2.24:M46/2
    Based on materials collected by the Division of Regional Medical Programs from its establishment in February 1966. First lists publications about individual regional programs (alphabetically by region) including those published by the programs themselves, nationally published books and journal articles, and those published by the Division. Second is a list of books and journal articles about regional medical programs in general.

DICTIONARIES

495. U.S. Public Health Service. **Emergency Health Services Glossary.** Washington, GPO, 1969. 101 p. $1.00. LC Card No. 71-603695. FS 2.302:A-10
    "This collection combines in a single reference document definitions and abbreviations relating to emergency health and medical services from 21 separate glossaries and other sources." Designed primarily for use by health and medical professional personnel and others concerned about or involved in the provision of emergency health services. Source symbol is given for each definition and a list of sources appears in the front of the book.

DIRECTORIES

496. U.S. National Institutes of Health. **Associate Training Programs in the Medical and Biological Sciences.** Washington, GPO, 1969. 75 p. Issuing Agency. LC Card No. 65-60919. FS 2.22:M46/4/969
    Its purpose is to "set forth in one place brief descriptions of programs of

concern to those interested in Associateships at the National Institutes of Health," and it is specifically directed toward those physicians and others "undertaking careers in medical or related research, or in academic medicine." Provides general and specific information on associateships.

STATISTICS

497. U.S. Public Health Service. **Health Manpower Source Book: Section 20, Manpower Supply and Educational Statistics for Selected Health Occupations: 1968.** Prep. by the Manpower Resources Staff. Washington, GPO, 1969. 164 p. $1.75. LC Card No. 52-61801. FS 2.2:M31/sec.20

This is a compilation of statistics on the supply and education of health manpower. It is arranged by occupation and covers each health profession for which educational support is available under the Health Professions Educational Assistance Act and the Nurse Training Act. Occupations include medicine, dentistry, optometry, pharmacy, podiatry, veterinary medicine, public health, and technicians including medical record librarianship. Data presented includes trends in number of schools and graduates, geographic distribution of schools, programs, students and graduates for a current year; trends in number of persons in the profession and in proportion to the population; and distribution of persons in the profession and ratios to the population for the current year by state. Also presents historical data back to the 19th century and projects some data to 1975. Supplements **Health Resources Statistics, 1968,** q.v.

498. U.S. Public Health Service. **Health Resources Statistics, Health Manpower and Health Facilities, 1968.** 2nd ed. Washington, GPO, 1968. 260 p. $2.50. LC Card No. 66-62580. FS 2.123:968

This statistical compendium of the health resources of the United States provides information on health manpower and facilities for planners, administrators, researchers, and those who are concerned with development of national, state, and regional health programs. The first section is on health manpower by types of service or occupational training. Part two covers inpatient health facilities. An appendix contains a list of health occupations. Indexed by subject.

DENTISTRY

499. U.S. National Institutes of Health, Division of Dental Health. **Directory of Prepaid Dental Care Plans, 1967.** By William B. Bock and Mary J. Sperberg. Washington, GPO, 1968. 309 p. Issuing Agency. LC Card No. 74-601029. FS 2.22:D43/12/967

"This directory includes only those privately sponsored prepaid dental plans reported to the Division of Dental Health," and is a compilation of data obtained from a survey conducted by the Division. It supersedes the 1963 **Digest of Prepaid Dental Care Plans.** Over 900 plans are arranged alphabetically within states. Entries include address, date of establishment, description, beneficiaries, and benefits. Also includes a brief list of definitions of prepaid dental care terms and a chart showing the scope of benefits.

500. U.S. National Library of Medicine. **Dentistry; a Selected List of Audio-visuals.** Washington, National Library of Medicine, 1968. 81 + 29 p. Issuing Agency. LC Card No. 71-603419. FS 2.211/3:D43

Lists slides and films available on different aspects of dentistry with pertinent physical information and detailed textual descriptions of each. Lists distributors with addresses.

501. U.S. Public Health Service. **The National Institute of Dental Research Directory of U.S. Facilities Providing Cleft Lip and Cleft Palate Services.** Washington, GPO, 1969. 270 p. Issuing Agency. LC Card No. 78-604056. FS 2.22: C58

The directory is designed to aid families who are seeking cleft palate services by providing a referral guide to directors of service facilities and other organizations. The main section lists centers alphabetically by cities under states. Information includes center's name, address, telephone number, director, date service started, services available, area and group served, and names of professional staff. Four tables in the front give statistical data on services.

MEDICINE

BIBLIOGRAPHIES

502. U.S. National Aeronautics and Space Administration. **Continuing Bibliography on Aerospace Medicine and Biology.** Springfield, Va., Clearinghouse, 1964— . Monthly. $3.00 each. LC Card No. 65-62677. NAS 1.21:7011(& nos.)

"Serves as a current abstracting and announcement medium for references on this subject," concentrating on biological, physiological, and environmental effects of real or simulated space flight. Includes three abstract sections: publications selected from STAR (**Scientific and Technical Aerospace Reports**), IAA (**International Aerospace Reports**), and LC entries (i.e. journal articles). Includes subject, personal author and corporate author indexes. Indexes refer to entry numbers in the abstract section. January issue each year is a cumulative index to the previous 11 issues. This publication is one of a series of technical and specialized bibliographies issued by NASA.

503a. U.S. National Clearinghouse for Smoking and Health. **Bibliography on Smoking and Health, With English Language Abstracts of Foreign Items, 1968 Cumulation.** Washington, GPO, 1968. 296 p. $2.00. LC Card No. 68-60300. FS 2.21:45/3

503b. U.S. National Clearinghouse for Smoking and Health. **Bibliography on Smoking and Health, With English Language Abstracts of Foreign Items, 1969 Cumulation.** Washington, GPO, 1969. 321 p. $2.75. FS 2.21:45/4

A catalog of materials added to the Library of the National Clearinghouse for Smoking and Health during 1967. Supplements the 1967 cumulation. Project was begun for the 1964 publication, **Smoking and Health, Report of the Advisory Committee to the Surgeon General of the Public Health Service.** Items were later added to support Clearinghouse programs and "for the general use of the scientific community." Arranged alphabetically within 11 categories, with a system of letters and numbers assigned each entry. Two indexes are necessary for use of this bibliography: Individual & Organization Index and Subject Index.

504. U.S. National Institute of Child Health and Human Development. **Film Guide on Reproduction and Development: A Guide to Selected Films on Reproduction and Developmental Biology for Graduate and Undergraduate Programs in the Biomedical Sciences.** Washington, GPO, 1969. 66 p. Illus. $1.25. LC Card No. 76-603672. FS 2.22/15:R29

Selected for their usefulness as teaching aids, these films are listed under six main topics and show title, physical description, producer, brief description, audience level, technical summary of contents, reviewers' comments, references to literature, distributor and purchase information, and accompanying materials including 16 mm versions available.

505. U.S. National Institutes of Health. **Epilepsy Abstracts; a Review of Published Literature, 1947-67.** Ed. by J.F. Mirandolle and L.M. Vencken. Washington, GPO, 1969. 2 vols. Issuing Agency. LC Card No. 70-604019. FS 2.22/59-2: 947-69/pt.1 & 2

This bibliography is concerned primarily with the clinical and therapeutic aspects of epilepsies, including research in physiology, biochemistry and the psychological, sociological and epidemiological aspects. Volume one contains the abstracts and gives the authors' names, titles of articles, journal titles, volumes, page numbers, and years of publication. Volume two contains author and subject indexes.

506. U.S. National Institutes of Health. **Fibrinolysis, Thrombolysis and Blood Clotting Bibliography, Annual Compilation, 1968.** Washington, GPO, 1969. 1153 p. Issuing Agency. LC Card No. 67-62840. FS 2.22/13-6:968

This is the 1968 cumulation of the monthly issues of this bibliography. Contains a subject section (with entries arranged under selected subject headings), author section (arranged by first author), subject index and author index. Citations were processed by MEDLARS.

507. U.S. National Library of Medicine. **An Annotated Bibliography of Biomedical Computer Applications.** Comp. by Ruth Allen. Washington, National Library of Medicine, 1969. 216 p. Issuing Agency. LC Card No. 76-602281. FS 2.209:B52/2

This bibliography was prepared by the Interuniversity Communications Council, Inc., under contract to the National Library of Medicine. Its purpose is to select and describe literature that encourages a more complete understanding of the computer as a research tool for the life sciences. Part I—Bibliographies; Part II—Books and Monographs; Part III—Articles from journals and monographs arranged under categories such as Biological Systems Analysis, Simulation, Medical

Records, etc.; Part IV—Author Index; and Part V—Subject Index.

508. U.S. National Library of Medicine. **Bibliography of the History of Medicine, No. 3, 1967.** Washington, GPO, 1969. 316 p. $2.75. LC Card No. 66-62950. FS 2.209/4:3

An annual bibliography of recent literature on the history of medicine and related sciences and professions. The series will be cumulated every five years. Number 1 (1965) is o.p.; No. 2 (1966) is available from GPO for $1.25.

All chronological periods and geographic areas are included. Covers journal articles, monographs, and analytic entries for symposia, congresses and similar composite publications, as well as historical chapters in general monographs. This volume covers material indexed but not necessarily published in 1967. The majority of the journal articles are from **Index Medicus** while monographs are from the **Current Catalog** which lists all monographs received in the National Library of Medicine. Additional citations were gathered and reviewed from other journals, bibliographies and recent publications. Arranged in four parts: Part I, Biographies—includes works dealing with medical history of famous non-medical persons, or with medical aspects of the work of literary figures, composers, etc., as well as those dealing with lives and contributions of medical people. Part II, Subject Index—lists the citations under subject headings. Part III, Authors— lists, alphabetically by author, citations appearing in Parts I and II. Part IV, Recent Acquisitions—lists by author only sixteenth century imprints received since completion of the **Catalogue of Sixteenth Century Printed Books in the National Library of Medicine** (1967).

509. U.S. Public Health Service. **Geronto-Psychiatric Literature in the Postwar Period: Review of the Literature to January 1, 1965.** By L. Ciompi. Washington, GPO, 1969. 97 p. $1.00. LC Card No. 70-601679. FS 2.22:G31/3/965

Translated from: **Fortschrifte der Neurologie Psychiatrie und Ihrer Grenzgebiete** (Stuttgart), 34(2):49-159, 1966.

A comprehensive "review of current thinking about aging." Contains 2747 citations, foreign and English, arranged alphabetically by author under broad subject headings. Tells where journal articles are abstracted if possible.

510. U.S. Public Health Service. **Readings on Cancer, An Annotated Bibliography.** Prep. by the Research Information Branch, National Cancer Institute. Washington, GPO, 1969. 23 p. $0.25. LC Card No. 70-600690. FS 2.21:14/4

A selective, briefly annotated bibliography designed to serve cancer patients, teachers, and students. 181 items are arranged by types: pamphlets, articles and books, plus a section on sources of information on cancer. Includes a topical index and a note to science teachers with a brief list of institutional materials. Items are graded.

DIRECTORIES

511. U.S. National Institutes of Health. **International Directory of Gerontology.**

Washington, GPO, 1969. 330 p. $2.30. LC Card No. 73-602267. FS 2.22: G31/4

This directory, prepared by the Gerontological Society, Inc. under a contract with the National Institute of Child Health and Human Development, provides biographical sketches of persons concerned with research on many different aspects of aging. Consists of three major parts. Part I: Biographies—U.S., arranged alphabetically by name, followed by a listing of biographies by state, list of gerontological institutions in the U.S. and special research resources. Part II: Biographies—Foreign, arranged alphabetically under 46 countries. Institutions and research resources are listed for each country after biographies. Part III lists persons by discipline within countries.

512. U.S. Public Health Service. Cancer Control Program. **Cancer Services: Facilities and Programs in the United States.** Rev. ed. Washington, GPO, 1969. 210 p. $1.25. LC Card No. 60-64681. FS 2.2:C16/5/968

The 1968 edition, published in 1969, is a revision and amplification of that issued for 1965. Contains a summary of cancer facilities and services available in each state and territory with an appendix of mortality statistics by state and type of cancer. Lists addresses and chief officers of state health departments, advisory groups, members of the cancer committees of state medical societies, cancer teaching coordinators, addresses of state divisions of the American Cancer Society, and other relevant associations.

513. U.S. National Clearinghouse for Smoking and Health. **Directory of on-Going Research in Smoking and Health.** Compiled by Herner and Company. 2nd ed. Washington, GPO, 1968. 375 p. "Free from PHS only." LC Card No. 67-61689. FS 2.2:Sm7/5/968

An "international directory of research studies dealing with the relationship between smoking and health . . . for use primarily by researchers in the field." The 364 projects represent 36 states, 25 foreign countries and the District of Columbia. Data was collected from the results of questionnaires sent to over 1,500 U.S. and foreign research workers and organizations. It is arranged alphabetically by name of the research organization. Project titles, principal investigators or researchers, objectives, methodologies, results to date, future plans, project dates, sources of financial support and bibliographical references are given for each. "Through its descriptions of on-going activities in the biomedical, behavioral, psychological and other fields . . ., this publication seeks to convey the growing scope and progress of research into the health hazards of smoking, as well as to help research entities coordinate their efforts." Concluded by four indexes: by subject, investigators, sponsors, and geographical locations.

PERIODICALS

514. U.S. National Institutes of Health. **Diabetes Literature Index.** Ed. by Arnold Lazarow and others. Washington, GPO, 1966- . Monthly. $4.00/yr. FS 2.22/53:vol. 3, 1968

Issued in cooperation with the American Diabetes Association and prepared cooperatively by the University of Minnesota, Case Western Reserve
University and the University of Rochester. A computer produced bibliography
from MEDLARS tapes which is designed to be "a specialized information medium . . . available free to qualified interested investigators and practitioners in
the field of diabetes." Indexes all current scientific papers relevant to the
field of diabetes from the world medical literature. Author and key word indexes give complete citations under each entry. Annual cumulations supercede
the 12 monthly issues.

515. U.S. National Institutes of Health. **Endocrinology Index.** Ed. by N.
Victoria Ragin. Washington, GPO, 1968- . Bimonthly. $16.00/yr. FS 2.22/48-2:
v. 1, 1968

Publications of the National Institute of Arthritis and Metabolic Diseases
from MEDLARS are incorporated into this selected bibliography which is intended "to supply those scientists working in the field of endocrinology with
a . . . current awareness tool and . . . to help facilitate greater integration of
research and clinical efforts in this field." Arranged in six sections: subjects,
by broad topics; reviews; methods; authors, alphabetically by the first author
of a study; subject index and author index, which includes all authors.

STATISTICS

516. U.S. Public Health Service. **Diabetes Source Book.** Prep. by Helen M.
Vavra. Washington, GPO, 1969. 80 p. $0.75. LC Card No. 74-604351.
FS 2.2:D54/13/968

A handy one-volume source providing statistical data on all the various
aspects of diabetes such as prevalence, associated factors, disability, etc. A useful source for researchers, students and those involved in the development of
effective public health programs in diabetes.

517. U.S. Public Health Service. **Use of Tobacco: Practices, Attitudes, Knowledge,
and Briefs, United States, Fall 1964 and Spring 1966.** By Dorothy E. Green and
others. Washington, GPO, 1969. 916 p. Issuing Agency. LC Card No. 78-604537.
FS 2.2:T55

A compendium of statistics on the incidence of tobacco use (particularly
smoking of cigarettes), attitudes toward the use of tobacco and other related
variables based on data collected in household interviews in the fall of 1964
and in the spring of 1966. Questions asked in the surveys are followed by the
statistics of responses. Includes sample interview schedules.

HANDICAPPED

518. U.S. Department of Health, Education and Welfare. Community and
Field Services. **Financial Assistance Programs for the Handicapped.** Washington, GPO, 1968. 98 p. $1.00. LC Card No. HEW 68-140. FS 1.6/3:H19

A guide to HEW's financial assistance programs for the handicapped.

Sixty-nine programs are listed under these major headings: (1) Basic and Supportive Services; (2) Research and Demonstration; (3) Construction; (4) Training; (5) Income Maintenance; and (6) Other. Provides purpose, eligibility requirements, address from which further information may be obtained, and authorizing legislation for each program.

519. U.S. Library of Congress. Division of the Blind and Physically Handicapped. **Books on Magnetic Tape.** Washington, Division of the Blind and Physically Handicapped, 1968. 48 p. Issuing Agency. LC 19.2:T16/2/no.1

A partial list of books and magazines on magnetic tape which are available from regional libraries for the blind and physically handicapped which cooperate with the Library of Congress in its program of "distributing braille and recorded reading materials on free loan to persons who are unable to read conventionally printed books because of a visual or physical disability." Arranged first by subject and then alphabetically by author, with a separate alphabetical author and title listing. A complete catalog of books and magazines on magnetic tape is planned.

520. U.S. President. **Guidebooks for Handicapped Travelers.** Washington, President's Committee on Employment of the Handicapped, 1968. 16 p. Issuing Agency. PrEx 1.10/8:T69

A listing of guide books available for handicapped travelers arranged by the state and city which are the subjects of the books. Gives addresses for obtaining guide books.

521. U.S. President. **Membership Directory, pt. 1: Committees.** Washington, President's Committee on Employment of the Handicapped, 1969. 91 p. Issuing Agency. PrEx 1.10:M51/pt.1

Lists names and addresses of executive committee members, associate members, advisory council members and members of the various standing committees of the President's Committee on Employment of the Handicapped.

MENTAL RETARDATION

522. U.S. Children's Bureau. **Selected Reading Suggestions for Parents of Mentally Retarded Children.** Comp. and ed. by Eleanor Ernst Timberg in collaboration with Kathryn Arning Gorham. Washington, Children's Bureau, 1968. 29 p. Issuing Agency. LC Card No. HEW 68-17. FS 17.212:M52

Includes the "more easily available and recent books and pamphlets which cover the areas of greatest interest to parents, as well as books and pamphlets which will be found in local libraries." Arranged by subjects with an author index.

523. U.S. Department of Health, Education and Welfare. Secretary's Committee on Mental Retardation. **Mental Retardation Publications of the Department of Health, Education and Welfare.** Washington, GPO, 1968- . Annual. Free (single copies). LC Card No. HEW 67-35. FS 1.18:M52/yr.

"Consists of publications of the U.S. Department of Health, Education and Welfare concerned with mental retardation." Arranged under broad subject headings. Includes a brief annotation and instructions for ordering each publication. Subject, author and abbreviated title indexes. The 1969 edition supersedes that of 1968.

524. U.S. Department of Health, Education and Welfare. Secretary's Committee on Mental Retardation. **Mental Retardation Activities of the U.S. Department of Health, Education and Welfare.** Washington, GPO, 1969. 85 p. $1.00. LC Card No. 62-61602. FS 1.23/5:969

This is the annual report of the Secretary's Committee on Mental Retardation, part two of which is a directory of mental retardation activities arranged under agencies of HEW. Gives details of the programs, the purposes and accomplishments of each during the previous year. It also provides organization charts for the Department and the Social and Rehabilitation Service Administration, statistics on finances of the program, and lists of authorizations for appropriations for mental retardation grants for past and future fiscal years.

MENTAL HEALTH

BIBLIOGRAPHIES

525. U.S. National Institute of Mental Health. **Bibliography on Suicide and Suicide Prevention: 1897-1957, 1958-67.** By Norman L. Farberow. Washington, GPO, 1969. 203 p. $1.75. FS 2.22/13:Su3

The purpose of this bibliography, a publication of the National Clearinghouse for Mental Health Information, is to "provide a single reference source for all publications now available to the concerned investigator" relating to suicide and suicide prevention. Contains two separate bibliographies. The first, 1897-1958, incorporates and expands the bibliography originally published by Farberow and Shneidmen, **The Cry for Help** (McGraw-Hill, 1961) to cover 2202 items. The starting date of 1897 was the publication date of the monumental work by Emile Durkheim, **Le Suicide.** The second list contains 1267 items for the period 1958-1967. Covers English and foreign language published materials plus unpublished doctoral dissertations and items from privately collected bibliographies. Omitted are most medical articles written for physicians dealing with medical, physiological and surgical issues. Numbered citations are arranged alphabetically by author and gives full bibliographical information. Author and subject index is provided for both bibliographies. Farberow is co-director of Suicide Prevention Center, Los Angeles.

526. U.S. National Institute of Mental Health. **The Comprehensive Community Mental Health Center: An Annotated Bibliography.** 6th ed. Washington, GPO, 1969. 41 p. $0.30. FS 2.22/13:M52/8

This edition of the bibliography on the community mental health center is prepared for psychiatrists, psychologists, social workers, nurses, and other professionals and represents a review of the literature in 45 mental health related journals from 1957 to 1968. The 147 numbered entries are arranged by author under 10 major subject areas such as: consultation and education, in-patient, out-patient, emergency services, rehabilitation, etc. Entries provide full bibliographic data and brief annotations. Author index.

527. U.S. National Institute of Mental Health. **Volunteer Services in Mental Health, An Annotated Bibliography, 1955-69.** Prep. by Francine Sabey. Washington, GPO, 1969. 96 p. $1.00. LC Card No. 75-604082. FS 2.22/13:V88

Arranged by specific settings in which volunteers work, e.g. settlement houses, psychiatric hospitals, clinics, etc. Types of materials include articles, books, proceedings, and reports. Entries give bibliographic details and annotations. Also includes research and statistical studies, and a list of bibliographies and directories. Indexed by authors.

528. U.S. Public Health Service. **Annotated Bibliography on Inservice Training for Allied Professionals and Nonprofessionals in Community Mental Health.** Rev. Washington, GPO, 1969. 49 p. $0.55. LC Card No. 78-601673. FS 2.24:M52

Bibliography of materials published between 1960 and 1967 pertaining to aspects of training physicians, nurses, school psychologists, teachers and special educators, clergy and others working in community mental health. Arranged by types of personnel with detailed annotations. Indexed by subject.

529. U.S. Public Health Service. **Annotated Bibliography on Inservice Training for Key Professionals in Community Mental Health.** Washington, GPO, 1969. 52 p. $0.60. LC Card No. 70-601774. FS 2.24:M52/3

Bibliography pertaining to inservice training of key professional personnel (e.g. psychiatrists, clinical psychologists, psychiatric social workers and nurses) for community mental health programs. Includes materials published from 1960 to 1967 with detailed annotations. Indexed by types of personnel and specific training concepts.

530. U.S. Public Health Service. **Annotated Bibliography on Inservice Training in Mental Health for Staff in Residential Institutions.** Washington, GPO, 1969. 24 p. $0.35. LC Card No. 73-601775. FS 2.24:M52/2

Bibliography on inservice mental health training for personnel in residential institutions including references on training in mental hospitals, institutions for the mentally retarded, child care residential institutions, and nursing homes. Classified subject arrangement with detailed annotations. Indexed by types of personnel and specific training concepts.

531. U.S. Public Health Service. **Consultation in Mental Health and Related Fields; a Reference Guide.** By Fortune V. Mannino. Washington, GPO, 1969. 105 p. $0.50. LC Card No. 70-604768. FS 2.22/13:M52/9

This bibliography of mental health consultation literature is arranged alphabetically by author under broad subject categories. It includes more

than 790 books, journal articles and conference proceedings with a separate
list of films related to consultation practice. Indexed by author.

532. U.S. Public Health Service. **Social Aspects of Alienation: An Annotated
Bibliography.** By Mary H. Lystad. Washington, GPO, 1969. 92 p. $1.00. LC
Card No. 74-604666. FS 2.22/13:Al4

"Alienation in the social sense is viewed as a sign of personal dissatisfaction
with the structural elements of modern society." This bibliography was published as a "first step towards the critical evaluation of the problem of alienation." It includes works on specific types of alienated people (e.g. youth,
black people), on methodology, culture change and deviant social behavior.
Complete bibliographical citations and very detailed annotations are given.
Indexed by authors.

DIRECTORIES

533. U.S. National Institute of Mental Health. Citizen Participation Branch.
College Student Volunteers in State Mental Hospitals. By Mary Cummins.
Washington, GPO, 1968. 30 p. $0.25. LC Card No. 68-61197. FS 2.22:M52/68

Partial results of a survey of college student volunteer programs in state
mental hospitals. First presents an overview of programs, then a list of the
hospitals (alphabetically by state) and the participating academic institutions.

534. U.S. Public Health Service. **Mental Health Training Grant Awards.** Prep.
by the Division of Manpower and Training Programs. Washington, GPO, 1968.
89 p. $0.45. FS 2.22/7-4:967

Arranged alphabetically by state and institution listing the grant number,
program area, number of trainees, amount of stipends, teaching costs and total
amount authorized for each program at each institution. A glossary lists the
major areas of training and their abbreviated titles as used in the directory.

535. U.S. Public Health Service. **Private Funds for Mental Health: An Annotated List of Foundations and Other Private Granting Agencies which Support
Research, Training or Services in Mental Health and Related Disciplines.** Prep.
by John E. Hinkle. Washington, GPO, 1969. 31 p. $0.25. LC Card No. 72-
604758. FS 2.22:M52/77

An "attempt to provide recent information to professionals and others
in the broad field of mental health about private sources of support available
for mental health activities." Arranged alphabetically by names of agencies
and foundations with addresses, types of support, fields of interest in mental
health, and relevant comments.

536. U.S. Public Health Service. **Selected Sources of Inexpensive Mental Health
Materials; A Directory for Mental Health Educators.** Washington, GPO, 1968.
70 p. $0.40. LC Card No. 76-603167. FS 2.22/13:M52/7

"Compiled to aid personnel responsible for planning, coordinating, or conducting mental health education programs." Includes publishers of mental health educational materials designed for use by the lay public and groups involved in educating the public and excludes trade or textbook publishers. Subject index at the front lists sources of information on subjects within the mental health field. The alphabetical listing of organizations provides a brief history and a listing of publications of each group.

NURSING

537. U.S. National Institutes of Health. **Schools Participating in Nursing Student Assistance Programs, Fiscal Year 1970.** Washington, GPO, 1969. 16 p. Issuing Agency. FS 2.22:N93/10/970

A directory which lists schools alphabetically by state with type of degree and city. Symbols denote those schools which participate in the Nursing Student Loan Program only or the Nursing Scholarship Program only.

538. U.S. Public Health Service. **Health Manpower Source Book: Section 2, Nursing Personnel.** Washington, GPO, 1969. 144 p. $1.50. HE 20.3109:2

Presents data on the number, distribution and characteristics of nursing personnel by state and geographic regions. Divided into eight sections with each section preceded by a discussion of the methods used in making estimates, evaluation of the reliability of sources and background material needed for accurate interpretation of the figures.

PHARMACOLOGY

539. U.S. Food and Drug Administration. Consumer Protection and Environmental Health Service. **National Drug Code Directory.** Prep. by the Science Information Facility. Washington, GPO, 1969. 338 p. $2.75. LC Card No. 76-604050. FS 13.134:969

"The first edition of the **National Drug Code Directory** represents the culmination of a two-year effort to establish a standardized, drug product identification system for the computer processing of drug information in the United States." It is essentially a computer-produced listing of over 12,000 prescription and over-the-counter drugs. The main section of the volume is organized alphabetically by product name with the name of the manufacturer and national drug code (an alpha-numeric code which denotes manufacturer, drug product and basic trade package size). The "Index of Established Names" refers from scientific names to the brand names in the main directory. The "National Drug Code Index" lists codes in numerical order with their product name and is thereby a listing of all products by manufacturer. Two appendixes provide supplementary information: The first is a directory of manufacturers by the short forms of their names with long forms and addresses; second is a prototype drug coding system for compounded prescriptions.

540. U.S. National Clearinghouse for Mental Health. **Bibliography of Drug Dependence and Abuse, 1928-1966.** Chevy Chase, Md., Clearinghouse, 1969. 158 p. Issuing Agency. LC Card No. 70-600726. FS 2.22/13:D84/928-66

This bibliography was compiled for the use of specialists and research workers and includes 3000 citations to books, monographs, articles, legal documents, and reports of congressional hearings. Material is arranged in eight groups: general reviews, incidence, sociological factors, treatment, attitudes and education, pharmacology and chemistry, psychological factors, and production, control and legal factors. Citations give full bibliographical details but no annotations.

541. U.S. National Institute of Mental Health. **Anti-Depressant Drug Studies 1955-1966: Bibliography and Selected Abstracts.** By Aaron Smith and others. Washington, GPO, 1969. 659 p. $5.50. LC Card No. 70-601845. FS 2.22/13: An8/955-66

Covers all reports concerning drugs used in treatment of psychiatric depression published in English from 1955 to 1966. Includes citations from 120 journals, 29 books and five other sources. Approximately one-half of the items listed include abstracts. At the front of the volume is a list of journals and other sources and an index of drugs. Two major parts: a complete bibliography arranged alphabetically by author with full bibliographic citation starred if abstracted, and abstracts arranged alphabetically by author.

542. U.S. Public Health Service. **Resource Book for Drug Abuse Education.** Washington, GPO, 1969. 117 p. $1.25. FS 2.22:D84/12

Contains summaries of factual information on the major drugs of abuse, and techniques and suggestions that drug educators have found helpful in communicating with young people thinking about or already experimenting with drugs. Includes papers by medical authorities and social scientists which reflect a wide range of views on drugs, and a section on planning drug abuse education workshops.

PUBLIC HEALTH

GENERAL WORKS

543. U.S. National Institutes of Health. **National Institutes of Health Almanac, 1969.** Bethesda, Md., NIH, 1969. 136 p. Issuing Agency. FS 2.22:A16/969

Intended to "offer in one volume all important historical data and other reference material" pertinent to the National Institutes of Health. Data is arranged within eight major sections: "Historical Data," including chronologies and biographical sketches; "The Organization," which explains the functions and contains a breakdown of the bureaucratic structure; "Appropriations," by types of awards; "Support of Medical Research," a statistical coverage of the federal government's role; "The Staff," showing numbers and types of personnel; "Real Property and Facilities," including locations and histories as well as pertinent statistical data; "Field Units," including overseas and domestic units; and "The Lecture Series," giving dates, titles, speakers, and place of each lecture in each series from its inception.

544a. U.S. National Institutes of Health. **National Institutes of Health Scientific Directory, 1968 and Annual Bibliography, 1967.** Washington, GPO, 1968. 243 p. $0.70. LC Card No. 57-62015. FS 2.21:75

544b. U.S. National Institutes of Health. **National Institutes of Health Scientific Directory, 1969 and Annual Bibliography, 1968.** Washington, GPO, 1969. 278 p. $1.25. LC Card No. 57-62015. FS 2.22/13-8:969

"Intended for reference use by research workers in the biomedical sciences," but will prove useful to anyone in the health fields. Includes an outline structure of the NIH, its professional staff and their scientific and technical publications, with the same information for the National Institute of Mental Health. Arranged by institute and division, and both directory and bibliographical entries are included together at the lower or branch level. Includes names of scientific staff members, other key individuals and visiting scientists and guest workers with a tenure of a year or more. Chiefs or heads of divisions are noted. Bibliography contains citations to the previous year's publications; directory is for the current year. Indexed by subjects and names.

545. U.S. Public Health Service. **Community Health Service Publications Catalog.** 1969 edition. Washington, GPO, 1969. 62 p. $0.35. LC Card No. 74-603082. FS 2.24:C73/2

Contains a listing of currently available publications related to activities and programs of the Community Health Service with some titles from other government and nongovernment sources. Publications are listed under 11 broad topics and are indexed by title.

546. U.S. Public Health Service. **Comprehensive Health Planning; A Selected Annotated Bibliography.** Washington, GPO, 1968. 31 p. $0.35. LC Card No. 68-61469. FS 2.24:H34/4

"Identifies and describes articles and publications which relate to comprehensive health planning." Publications from 1965 to May 1967 are included. Out-of-print materials are so noted. Numbered entries are arranged alphabetically within six broad categories. An author/editor index refers to entry numbers. Includes addresses of both governmental and private publishers and of relevant associations.

547. U.S. Public Health Service. **Current Literature on Venereal Disease; Abstracts and Bibliography.** Washington, Public Health Service, 1966- . 3 or 4 times/yr. Issuing Agency. FS 2.11/2:date/issue no.

"Presents a survey of recently published literature in the field." Annotations are descriptive and written with the purpose of enabling the reader to decide whether the original article would be of interest to him. Arranged under three main areas: diagnosis and management; research and evaluation; and public health methods. Includes annual author and subject indexes; individual issues are not indexed. The MEDLARS system was first used in compiling the second issue of the 1968 bibliography.

548. U.S. Public Health Service. **Public Health Engineering Abstracts.** Washington, GPO, 1928- . Monthly. LC Card No. 70-600422. FS 2.13:47

A monthly review of more than 800 domestic and foreign journals of science and engineering, reports of states and the federal government, and reports and proceedings of scientific research groups. "Articles abstracted are selected for their relationship and importance to environmental health." Entries are arranged alphabetically by author under broad subjects. Two indexes are published annually—author and subject.

549. U.S. Public Health Service. **Publications of the Health Facilities Planning and Construction Service, Hill-Burton Program.** Rev. Washington, GPO, 1968. 35 p. $0.30. FS 2.74/3:G-3/5

Lists available publications only. Not retrospective and not indexed.

550. U.S. Public Health Service. **Selected References on Group Practice.** Washington, GPO, 1968. 29 p. Issuing Agency. FS 2.24:G91

First of what is planned to be a series of materials on the subject of group practice of medicine. Includes articles and books on organizational techniques and structure, the legal and economic aspects, administration, quality of care and research. Arranged alphabetically by author under subjects. Includes a list of annual reports issued by selected medical groups and a list of periodicals containing many articles on the subject. Entries are not annotated. No index.

551. U.S. Public Health Service. **Training Methodology; an Annotated Bibliography.** Washington, GPO, 1969. 4 pts. $3.75. LC Card No. 70-601777. FS 2.24:T68/pts.1-4

Part 1: **Background Theory and Research.** 90 p. $1.00. Pertains to research and theory on individual behavior, group behavior, and educational and training philosophy.

Part 2: **Planning and Administration.** 119 p. $1.00. Pertains to aspects of instructional design, course planning, and training program administration.

Part 3: **Instructional Methods and Techniques.** 100 p. $1.00. Pertains to specific instruction methods and techniques for both individuals and groups.

Part 4: **Audiovisual Theory, Aids and·Equipment.** 80 p. $0.75. Pertains to the media aspects of training with reference on audiovisual theory and methods, aids, facilities and equipment.

Each volume is arranged by broad subjects with detailed annotations for each entry and is indexed by specific subjects.

DIRECTORIES

552. U.S. Consumer Protection and Environmental Health Service. **Public Advisory Committees: Authority, Structure, Functions, Members.** Washington,

GPO, 1969. 128 p. Issuing Agency. LC Card No. 62-61159. HE 20.1009:969

A directory of the personnel and functions of public committees which serve as advisors to the Public Health Service's Consumer Protection and Environmental Health Service. Committees are listed for the Environmental Control Administration, the Food and Drug Administration, and the National Air Pollution Control Administration, including authority, structure, functions, meetings and lists of members of each. Two indexes list the committees and the members alphabetically.

553. U.S. Public Health Service. **A Directory of National Organizations with an Interest in School Health.** 5th ed. Washington, Public Health Service, 1968. 30 p. Issuing Agency. LC Card No. 68-67055. FS 2.2:Sch6/5

Lists 88 organizations working for more effective utilization of available school health resources in a wide range of fields (e.g. deaf education, guidance, drug abuse, mental health, dentistry). Arranged alphabetically by name with headquarter's address and telephone number and name of executive officer for each.

554. U.S. Public Health Service. **Directory of State, Territorial, and Regional Health Authorities, 1968.** Washington, GPO, 1969. 147 p. $1.25. LC Card No. 24-26996. FS 2.77/2:969

This annual directory provides information useful to those administering grant programs of the Health Services and Mental Health Administration and the Crippled Children's Service of the Social and Rehabilitation Service. The 1968 edition was enlarged to include a section concerning administration of regional medical programs; also includes information about principal health authorities and health departments. Lists health officers by state, by units of comprehensive health planning agencies, and lists regional medical programs, state agencies administering Crippled Children's Service Programs, state agencies administering Hospital and Medical Facilities Construction Programs, and those administering Mental Health Programs.

555. U.S. Public Health Service. **1969 Directory of Migrant Health Projects Assisted by Public Health Service Grants.** Washington, Health Services and Mental Health Administration, 1969. 178 p. Issuing Agency. LC Card No. 70-602348. FS 2.2:M58/6/969

Projects are listed by grant number under states. Entries give project, sponsor, director, span of migrant season, estimated number of migrants, counties served, health services provided, and location of family health service centers. Includes programs in 36 states and Puerto Rico. Maps at the beginning of each state section show all the migrant-impacted counties, and which counties provide both personal health care and sanitation services.

LAWS

556. U.S. Public Health Service. **Compendium of State Statutes on the Regulation of Ambulance Services, Operation of Emergency Vehicles and Good**

Samaritan Laws. Rev. ed. Washington, GPO, 1969. unpaged. $1.50. FS 2.302: A-11

This compendium is current to May 1969 and provides a summary table of laws for all states, followed by material arranged alphabetically by state, citing laws and dates enacted, and providing quotations from sections of the laws relating to emergency vehicles and services.

557. U.S. Bureau of Labor Standards. **Directory and Index of Safety and Health Laws and Codes.** Prep. by Richard M. Bonk and Thomas H. Seymour. Washington, GPO, 1969. 109 p. $1.25. LC Card No. 77-603281. L 16.2: Sa1/31

Compiles "under one cover all known occupational safety and health regulations and laws administered by the States." Arranged by states with a subject index and a classified index which groups various subjects under one heading and gives an overall picture of the laws in various states. Does not give the full law but rather the statute numbers and administrative codes, rules and regulations.

TOXICOLOGY

558. U.S. Library of Congress. National Referral Center for Science and Technology. **A Directory of Information Resources in the United States: General Toxicology.** Washington, GPO, 1969. 293 p. $4.00. LC Card No. 73-602563. LC 1.31:D62/5

Compiled by the National Referral Center for Science and Technology with the assistance of the Toxicology Information Program of the National Library of Medicine.

"Planned to provide a ready reference tool for identifying toxicological information resources in the United States," and is representative of the "various sources of toxiciology-related information in the United States." Excludes general libraries and individuals. Arranged alphabetically by sponsoring agency. Gives address, specific areas of interest, library holdings, publications, and information services available. Three valuable appendixes are included: "Poison Control Centers," "Some United States Professional Organizations having Substantial Interest in Toxicology," and "Some United States Periodicials of Toxicological Interest." Subject and geographical indexes.

559. U.S. National Agricultural Library. **Toxicity of Herbicides to Mammals, Aquatic Life, Soil Microorganisms, Beneficial Insects and Cultivated Plans, 1950-65: a Selected List of References.** Comp. by Patricia A. Condon. Washington, National Agricultural Library, 1968. 161 p. (Library List no. 87). Issuing Agency. LC Card No. Agr68-196. A 17.17:87

560. U.S. National Library of Medicine. **Toxicity Bibliography.** Washington, GPO, 1968- . Quarterly. $9.00/yr. FS 2.218:v.nos. & nos.

A highly specialized medical bibliography which includes the "entire range of chemical and biological interactions" and is drawn selectively from current citations in the MEDLARS files. Covers reports on toxicity studies, adverse drug reactions, and poisoning in man and animals. Designed to provide "health professionals working in toxicology and related disciplines access to the world's relevant and significant journal literature in this field." Section I, Drugs and Chemicals, is by entry number with its own author and subject index. Section II, Adverse Reactions to Drugs and Chemicals, is subdivided by many categories with no index.

TRANSPORTATION

DIRECTORIES

561. U.S. Department of Housing and Urban Development. **Directory of Urban Transportation and Planning Projects.** Washington, GPO, 1969. 45 p. $0.55. HH 1.28:92

Contains summaries of urban transportation projects administered by HUD under the Urban Mass Transportation Act of 1964 as amended. The directory is divided into four areas: research and demonstration projects; technical studies; education, research and training grants; and HUD study of new systems of urban transportation. In the first three, projects are listed by state and title; in the fourth, by title. Gives project number, title, descriptions, grantee, approval date, estimated completion date, project cost and address for each. Indexed by type of project.

562. U.S. Bureau of Public Roads. **Directory, Urbanized Area Transportation Planning Programs.** Washington, Bureau of Public Roads, 1968. 50 p. Issuing Agency. TD 2.102:Ur1/968

Lists the comprehensive continuing transportation planning programs carried on cooperatively by state highway departments and the affected local governing bodies. Section one is by state with name, address and telephone number, key official and title of each program. Section two lists Federal Highway Administration Regional Planning and Research engineers and Urban Transportation Planning engineers. Section three lists Bureau of Public Roads Division planning and research engineers and state highway department planning officials.

AVIATION

563. U.S. Federal Aviation Administration. **Air Traffic and Airport Congestion, Selected References.** Comp. by Nancy B. Nelsen. Springfield, Va., CFSTI, 1969. 39 p. $3.00. LC Card No. 78-601787. TD 4.17/3:17

564. U.S. Federal Aviation Administration. **Census of U.S. Civil Aircraft, as of December 31, 1968.** By Sylvia Goring. Washington, GPO, 1969. 173 p. $1.50. LC Card No. 74-601175. TD 4.18:968

Contains the annual count of all registered civil aircraft in the United States. Lists aircraft by registration number, including the following information—manufacturer's serial number, make, model and type, number of engines, their make, model and type, data of aircraft inspection and type of registrant.

565. U.S. Federal Aviation Administration. **FAA Publications, 1969.** Washington, GPO, 1969. 27 p. Free from FAA. TD 4.17:969

"A catalog of selected printed materials which may be of interest to the public, to pilots and to the aviation industry." Arranged under broad subject categories, with instructions for ordering.

566. U.S. Federal Aviation Administration. **FAA Statistical Handbook of Aviation.** Prep. by Sylvia M. Goring. Washington, GPO, 1968. 274 p. Illus. $2.75. LC Card No. 46-26093. TD 4.20:968

"Designed to serve as a convenient source for historical data, and to assist in evaluating progress, determining trends, and estimating future activity." Contains charts, graphs and narrative descriptions of U.S. aviation activity including airports, aircraft and airmen, aeronautical products and exports, accidents and general aviation. Includes a glossary and a detailed subject index.

567. U.S. Library of Congress. **Wilbur and Orville Wright: A Bibliography Commemorating the 100th Anniversary of the Birth of Wilbur Wright, April 16, 1867.** Comp. by Arthur G. Renstrom. Washington, GPO, 1968. 187 p. $0.55. LC Card No. 68-60013. LC 33.2:W93

Issued as a "bibliographic service to scholars and others interested in aeronautical history . . . and also as a tribute . . . to Wilbur and Orville Wright by the Library of Congress." This bibliography is an expansion of the **Papers of the Wright Brothers** published in 1953 by McGraw-Hill. Arranged first by broad subject headings (e.g. Interviews, Aeroplanes and Flights, Juvenile Publications), and then, in most sections, chronologically. Annotated. Indexed by authors, persons, and institutions.

HIGHWAYS

568. U.S. Bureau of Public Roads. **Highway Statistics.** Washington, GPO, 1969. 191 p. $1.75. LC Card No. 47-32330. TD 2.110:968

1967 edition published in 1969 presents "1967 statistics and analytical tables of general interest on motor fuel, motor vehicles, driver licensing, highway user taxation, state highway finance, highway mileage, and Federal aid for highways; and 1966 highway finance data for municipalities, counties, townships, and other units of local government."

Historical highway statistics are contained in **Highway Statistics, Summary to 1965.**

569. U.S. Bureau of Public Roads. **Literature References to Highways and their Environmental Considerations.** Washington, Bureau of Public Roads, 1969. 80 p Issuing Agency. LC Card No. 71-603293. TD 2.123:L71

This bibliography is arranged under six broad areas of environmental considerations of highway design and planning with cross references to related areas. Indexed by subjects.

570. U.S. Federal Highway Administration. **Federal Highway Administration Publications.** Washington, Federal Highway Administration, 1969. 5 p. Issuing Agency. TD 2.10:P96/969

571. U.S. National Highway Safety Bureau. **Highway Safety Literature; Announcement of Recent Acquisitions.** Washington, National Highway Safety Bureau, 1969. Weekly issues. Issuing Agency. TD 2.210:nos.

Lists the recent acquisitions of the National Highway Safety Bureau's Documentation Center. Includes publications in all phases of highway or traffic safety. Arranged by subject with no index. Entries include accession numbers, corporate author, report title, personal author, date and number of pages with a brief abstract.

PART THREE

HUMANITIES

HUMANITIES

GENERAL WORKS

572. U.S. National Endowment for the Arts. **Programs of the National Endowment for the Arts through October 1969.** Washington, GPO, 1969. 63 p. Issuing Agency. LC Card No. 70-605008. NF 2.2:P94/4/969-3

Lists grants by fields of interest (e.g. architecture, dance, theatre, music). Gives current programs first and tells to whom award was given, present status of the work and amount awarded. List of completed programs gives the same type of information.

573. U.S. National Endowment for the Humanities. **Division of Research and Publication Handbook, 1968-69.** Washington, NEH, 1968. 12 p. Issuing Agency. NF 3.8:R31/968-69

The term humanities, as defined in the National Foundation on the Arts and Humanities Act of 1965, "includes, but is not limited to, the study of the following: language, both modern and classical; linguistics; literature; history; jurisprudence; philosophy; archaeology; the history, criticism, theory and practice of the arts; and those aspects of the social sciences which have humanistic content and employ humanistic methods." This handbook describes the scope, purpose and procedures of the National Endowment for the Humanities' Division of Research and Publication which supports research and scholarship in the humanities. It lists types of programs eligible for support (and those ineligible), tells how application should be made and what should be included, type of proposal to be submitted, how applications are evaluated, and how grants are administered. Includes an address for further inquiries.

574. U.S. National Endowment for the Humanities. **Program Information, 1969.** Washington, GPO, 1968. 7 p. Issuing Agency. NF 3.2:P94/2/969

Describes the purposes of the National Endowment for the Humanities (NEH) and the areas of study it supports. The four major programs (i.e. education program, public program, research program, and fellowship program) are discussed in detail and addresses are provided for those wishing further information. Also lists areas not funded by the NEH.

APPLIED ARTS

FASHIONS & FABRICS

575. U.S. National Museum. **Natural Dyes in the United States.** By Rita J. Adrosko. Washington, GPO (Smithsonian Institution Press), 1968. 160 p. Illus. $3.25. LC Card No. 70-600039. SI 3.3:281

The first section of this work is a discussion of dyes used in America during the 18th and 19th centuries. Chapter divisions are by colors. Part two contains recipes for home dyeing with natural dyes including information on color variations, fibers and necessary equipment. Includes a lengthy bibliography of general works, dye manuals and books printed in America before 1870 which contain a section of dye recipes. Appendixes contain excerpts from important early works on dyeing and a list of common names of chemicals used in dyeing. Indexed.

576. U.S. National Museum. **Women's Bathing and Swimming Costumes in the United States.** By Claudia B. Kidwell. Washington, GPO, 1969. 32 p. Illus. $0.50. LC Card No. 70-600054. SI 3.3:250

Traces the evolution of women's swim fashions from colonial times to the present. Drawings and photographs further illustrate the changes from bathing dresses to swimming suits. A useful tool for students of fashion and cultural history. Indexed by persons and subjects.

FINE ARTS

577. U.S. Library of Congress. Reference Department. Prints and Photographs Division. **Catalog of the 21st National Exhibition of Prints Held at the Library of Congress, May 1-September 2, 1969.** Washington, GPO, 1969. 16 p. Illus. Issuing Agency. LC Card No. 43-16468. LC 25.8:969

Lists prints made after January 1, 1967 by artists residing in the United States and accepted by a panel of judges for showing in the 21st National Exhibition of Prints. Arranged alphabetically by artists with addresses, titles of prints, media and costs. Eight prints from the exhibit are reproduced in the catalog.

578. U.S. National Collection of Fine Arts. **Highlights of the National Collection of Fine Arts.** Designed by Stephen Kraft. Washington, Smithsonian Institution Press (Printed by Vinmar Lithographing Company), 1968. 64 p. Issuing Agency. LC Card No. 68-60063. SI 6.2:H54

Contains a brief history and outline of the development of the National Collection of Fine Arts with chapters on (1) 18th and 19th century painting, (2) 20th century painting, and (3) prints, drawings and watercolors in the Collection. Sample works are reproduced and discussed "to whet the appetite of the student to inquire further as to what other works are to be found . . ., to arouse the curiosity of the scholar and to please the casual visitor." Both the artist and the subject of the work depicted are discussed in most cases. Indexed by titles and artists.

579. U.S. National Collection of Fine Arts. **National Collection of Fine Arts, National Portrait Gallery: Museums of the Smithsonian Institution.** Washington, GPO, 1969. 16 p. Illus. $0.25. SI 6.2:N21/2/969

Describes the history and physical aspects of the building in Washington, D.C. which houses the National Portrait Gallery and the National Collection of Fine Arts. Includes a bibliography of references used.

580. U.S. National Collection of Fine Arts. **Presidential Portraits.** Comp. and written by Virginia C. Purdy and Daniel J. Reed. Ed. by J. Benjamin Townsend. Washington, National Collection of Fine Arts, 1968. 76 p. Issuing Agency. LC Card No. 68-55302. SI 11.2:P92

Gives a brief biography and physical description of each president plus a photograph of the presidential portrait and physical description of it (i.e. size, medium, year painted, and present owner).

581. U.S. National Collection of Fine Arts. **Sao Paulo 9, United States of America, Estados da America, Edward Hopper and Environment U.S.A. 1957-67.** By William C. Seitz and Lloyd Goodrich. Washington, Smithsonian Institution Press, 1968. 165 p. Illus. $10.00 (cloth), $5.95 (paper). LC Card No. 67-29477. SI 6.2:Sa6

582. U.S. National Collection of Fine Arts. **Werner Drewes Woodcuts Catalogue.** By Caril Dreyfuss. Washington, GPO, 1969. 32 p. Illus. $0.50. LC Card No. 70-603440. SI 6.2:D82

583. U.S. National Gallery of Art. **Brief Guide to the National Gallery of Art of the United States of America.** Washington, GPO, 1969. 32 p. Illus. Issuing Agency. SI 8.8:N21/969

A handy guide for visitors to the National Gallery of Art giving visiting hours, rules of the Gallery, locations of various rooms, and a history and description of the building. A guide to the exhibits includes floor plans and photographs of some of the art works.

584. U.S. National Gallery of Art. **Catalogue of Color Reproductions, Books and Catalogues, Educational Materials from the Publications Fund, National Gallery of Art.** Washington, National Gallery of Art, 1969. 58 p. Issuing Agency. LC Card No. 74-601857. SI 8.2:C28

Lists reproductions of famous art works, laminated plaques, color post cards, catalogs of major individual permanent collections in the National Gallery of Art, books and pamphlets, records, jewelry, and educational materials which are available from the National Gallery of Art.

585a. U.S. National Gallery of Art. **Report and Studies in the History of Art, 1967.** Washington, GPO, 1968. 145 p. Illus. $2.00. LC Card No. 68-60053. SI 8.9:967

585b. U.S. National Gallery of Art. **Report and Studies in the History of Art, 1968.** Washington, GPO, 1969. 235 p. Illus. $2.75. LC Card No. 68-60053. SI 8.9:968

A number of studies in the history of art are published here together with the report of the National Gallery of Art for the fiscal year. The report includes lists of acquisitions of the Gallery, of publications, donors, visiting lecturers, paintings on extended loan, exhibitions, and statistics of the various National Gallery of Art departments. A comprehensive source for information on the current activities of the National Gallery of Art.

586. U.S. National Portrait Gallery. **A Nineteenth-Century Gallery of Distinguished Americans.** Catalogue by Robert G. Stewart. Published for the National Portrait Gallery by the Smithsonian Institution Press. Washington, GPO, 1969. 93 p. Ports., $1.75. LC Card No. 70-600300. SI 11.2:Am3

A catalog of an exhibition from February 22 to May 1, 1969 at the National Portrait Gallery. Presents engraved reproductions of 147 of the original portraits used in James Barton Longacre and James Herring's **The National Portrait Gallery of Distinguished Americans** (4 v., 1834-39). The black and white portraits are accompanied by biographical notes and descriptions of the engravings and original drawings. Portraits are listed in alphabetical order. Indexes artists and engravers and provides a selected bibliography.

587. U.S. Smithsonian Institution. **Armed Forces of the United States as Seen by the Contemporary Artist.** Washington, GPO, 1968. 66 p. Illus. $0.65. LC Card No. 68-60820. SI 1.2:Ar5

This publication is a catalog of an exhibition by the National Armed Forces Museum Advisory Board and includes "representative works by 85 artists depicting all branches of the Armed Forces." The exhibit contained works by both civilian and military artists. The catalog lists works alphabetically by artist with a brief biographical sketch of each. For each work of art it lists title, media, size and permanent location. Black and white photographs of many works are also included in this catalog.

588. U.S. Smithsonian Institution. **Art Treasures of Turkey Circulated by the Smithsonian Institution, 1966-68.** By Richard Ettinghausen and others. Washington, Smithsonian Institution Press (Produced by Meriden Gravure Company and Connecticut Printers), (1966) 1968. 120 p. $10.00. LC Card No. 66-61710. SI 1.2:T84

The exhibition, Art Treasures of Turkey, was the "result of years of cooperative efforts by government officials, museum curators, scholars and experts in both Turkey and the United States, [and is] a comprehensive and representative survey of the many cultures that have flourished almost continuously in Anatolia since the neolithic age, and of treasures created and amassed in the former capital city, Istanbul." Contains narrative introductions and many photographs of art works from the following periods: (1) the Art of Anatolia until ca. 1200 BC; (2) Early Iron Age, Classical and Roman Empire; (3) the Byzantine Period; and (4) the Islamic Period. Each narrative section is followed by lengthy bibliographies. The catalog entries for the 282 works are numbered and include physical description of the work, date, lending museum and its accession number.

589. U.S. Smithsonian Institution. **Graphic Art of Mary Cassat.** Intro. by Adelyn D. Breeskin; forward by Donald H. Karshan. Washington, Smithsonian

Institution Press and Museum of Graphic Art, 1968. 112 p. $8.50. LC Card
No. 67-30432. SI 1.2:C27

LITERATURE

590. U.S. Library of Congress. **Carl Sandburg.** By Mark Van Doren. Washington, GPO, 1969. 83 p. $0.50. LC Card No. 71-600851. LC 19.9:V28

This document contains the text of Mark Van Doren's lecture at the
Library of Congress on January 8, 1968 as part of the Gertrude Clark Wittal
series and a 64 page bibliography of Sandburg materials in the Library of Congress. The bibliography, prepared by the Library of Congress staff, lists published and unpublished sources, manuscripts and audio-visual materials. It
excludes works about Sandburg.

591. U.S. Library of Congress. **Louisa May Alcott, A Centennial for Little
Women, An Annotated Selected Bibliography.** Comp. by Judith C. Ullom.
Washington, GPO, 1969. 91 p. Illus. $0.55. LC Card No. 76-600591.
LC 2.2:A11/2

This illustrated bibliography serves as a catalog of the Library of Congress
centennial exhibition for **Little Women** (1868). Contents: Early Writings, Novels,
Little Women Series, Multi-Volume Collections, Single-Volume Collections, Separate editions of Stories, Collections, Modern Anthologies, Bio-Critical Studies,
and a title index. This is a selective bibliography and contains only first editions
and some later editions which are significant for the illustrations.

592. U.S. Library of Congress. **Metaphor as Pure Adventure.** By James Dickey.
Washington, GPO, 1968. 20 p. $0.25. LC Card No. 68-61809. LC 1.14:D55/2

This publication contains the text of a lecture delivered at the Library of
Congress on December 4, 1967 by James Dickey, Consultant in Poetry in English
at the Library of Congress, 1966-68 and a bibliography of other publications on
literature issued by the Library of Congress. The bibliography is alphabetical by
title with date, page, cost and brief annotations.

593. U.S. Library of Congress. Subject Cataloging Division. **Subject Headings
for Children's Literature.** Washington, GPO, 1969. 30 p. $0.75 (from Subject
Cataloging Division, Processing Department). LC Card No. 76-602013. LC 26.2:
Su1/2

This is the statement of rules governing Library of Congress cataloging of
children's literature and a list of those subject headings for children's literature
which vary from those used for adult literature. Symbols indicate modified LC
headings and Sears headings (lack of symbol denotes a new heading).

MUSIC

594. U.S. Library of Congress. Reference Department. Music Division. **Sousa
Band, a Discography.** Compiled by James R. Smart. Washington, GPO, 1969.
123 p. $1.50. LC Card No. 70-604228. LC 12.2:So8

The purpose of this work is to "present in one source the recording history of the Sousa Band." It also includes recordings made by the U.S. Marine Band during the last three years of Sousa's leadership (1890-92) and the Philadelphia Rapid Transit Company Band which recorded two compositions under Sousa's direction. Recordings by the Sousa Band are listed first under one of two headings: cylinder records and disc records, and second alphabetically by title under record manufacturer. Excludes foreign releases of Sousa Band records. The exclusion of a title index makes it necessary for one to peruse the list of recordings of each individual company (as well as lists for the other two bands) in order to locate a specific title. The appendix contains a chronological list of Victor recording sessions. Indexed by soloists, composers, and conductors by companies.

595. U.S. National Museum. Division of Musical Instruments. **Harpsichords and Clavichords.** By Cynthia A. Hoover. Washington, GPO, 1969. 43 p. Illus. $0.40. LC Card No. 73-605896. SI 3.2:H23

Describes the restored harpsichords and clavichords which are occasionally on exhibit at the Hall of Musical Instruments of the Smithsonian Institution or in use in the concert series sponsored by the Division of Musical Instruments. The descriptions include year made, name and city of designer/maker, and physical aspects such as range, size, and number of sets of strings. Includes black-and-white photographs of each and a selected bibliography.

POPULAR CUSTOMS

596. U.S. Bureau of International Commerce. **Holidays Around the World Listed: A Guide for Business Travel.** Washington, GPO, 1969. 27 p. $0.20. C 42.8/1:H717/2/970

Pinpoints observance in 115 countries that close business and government offices. Arranged alphabetically by country within the five geographic regions of Europe, Western Hemisphere, Africa, Far East and Near East/South Asia.

MISCELLANEOUS

EXHIBITIONS

597. U.S. Travel Service. **United States Conventions and Exhibitions.** Washington, GPO, 1969. 36 p. Issuing Agency. C 47.2:C76/969

Lists over 100 conventions and is intended as a guide only. Includes only those organizations' conventions which responded to a U.S. Travel Service questionnaire saying that they welcome attendance from abroad at their meeting. Index by classifications, plus a chronological listing. The main body of the directory is by subject. Shows executive officer and address with a brief statement about the organization itself. Gives place and dates of conventions for current and forthcoming years.

GOVERNMENT PUBLICATIONS

598. U.S. Public Documents Division. **Monthly Catalog of United States**

Government Publications: Decennial Cumulative Index 1951-60; Index to Monthly Issues from January 1951 to December 1960. Washington, GPO, 1968. 2 v. $50.00. LC Card No. 4-18088. GP 3.8/3:951-60/v.1&2

Cumulates the annual indexes to the **Monthly Catalog** with references to the specific year and item number.

NAMES

599. U.S. Immigration and Naturalization Service. **Foreign Versions, Variations and Diminutives of English Names, Foreign Equivalents of United States Military and Civilian Titles.** Washington, GPO, 1969. 53 p. $1.00. J 21.2: N15/969

Designed to aid the person who needs to know the foreign equivalent of commonly used English given names and the foreign equivalents of U.S. military and civilian titles.

PERIODICALS

600. U.S. Library of Congress. **New Serial Titles, Union List of Serials Commencing Publication after December 31, 1949; 1966-67 Cumulation.** Washington, Library of Congress, 1968. 1733 p. $115.00/yr. LC Card No. 53-60021. LC 1.23/3:966-67

Supplements the third edition of the **Union List of Serials** for the years 1966 and 1967 and supercedes the 1966 cumulation. Lists periodicals which began publication in 1966 and 1967 with place of publication and holdings in U.S. and Canadian libraries. A section at the back lists title changes and periodicals which ceased publication during the period. Kept up-to-date by monthly issues, and annual cumulations.

601. U.S. Library of Congress. Reference Department. **Newspapers Currently Received and Permanently Retained in the Library of Congress.** Compiled by the Serials Division. Washington, GPO, 1968. 26 p. $0.35. LC Card No. 68-61877. LC 6.7:968

In two sections: U.S. and foreign. The U.S. section lists 255 newspapers by state and city; the foreign section, 876 papers by country and city. Unless otherwise noted, all newspapers are permanently retained by the Library of Congress. Titles in Oriental and Slavic languages are transliterated for entry here but are not translated. Note is made of those newspapers for which microfilm only is received.

PRINTING AND PUBLISHING

602. U.S. Government Printing Office. **GPO Standard Ink Book.** Washington, GPO, 1969. 230 p. $6.00. LC Card No. 75-606044. GP 1.2:In5/2/969

This book was developed as a "working tool in selecting printing inks for use by the Government Printing Office or procured through commercial contracts." It is printed on both coated and uncoated paper to show how paper finish affects colors. Selection of colors for this book was based on those "most often requested by the customer agencies and printed by the GPO." Except for the first two pages, this book consists entirely of illustrations of ink colors.

603. U.S. Government Printing Office. **Specimens of Type Faces.** Washington, GPO, 1969. 350 p. Illus. $5.00. LC Card No. 79-604651. GP 1.2:T98/11/969

This was published to familiarize patrons of the Government Printing Office with a new classification of typefaces and serves as a guide to typeset facilities and typefaces. It is a catalog of typefaces used in the Government Printing Office and includes GPO typeface classification system conversion instructions, instructions for selecting typefaces, mixing faces and copyfitting. Indexed by name of type (alphabetical) and by case numbers, and includes a glossary of printing terms.

WORD DIVISION

604. U.S. Government Printing Office. **Word Division; Supplement to the Government Printing Office Style Manual.** 7th ed. Washington, GPO, 1968. 190 p. $0.50. GP 1.2:W89/3/968

The **GPO Style Manual** is a standard tool designed to achieve uniform word and type treatment of government publications. This supplement on line-end word division is a quick reference aid for finding correct wordbreaks and spelling. It attempts to "lay down wordbreak rules based on generally accepted orthographic principles, pronounceable parts, and also on customs derived from good printing practices, particularly rules of good spacing." Follows the word divisions used by **Webster's Unabridged Dictionary,** 3rd ed., for the most part. The introduction lists GPO's 41 rules of style regarding wordbreaks. The body of the work consists of two-column pages of words with hyphens to indicate wordbreaks.

APPENDIX A

BIBLIOGRAPHIC SOURCES

GENERAL PUBLICATIONS

The major current bibliographic sources for government publications of general interest are the **Monthly Catalog of United States Government Publications, Selected United States Government Publications, Price Lists** and the publications lists of the various departments and agencies.

The **Monthly Catalog of United States Government Publications** is the most complete listing of government documents. Publications are listed under issuing agencies and indexed by subjects, personal names and sometimes by titles. Symbols are used in each entry to indicate the availability of documents: An asterisk (∗) means a publication is for sale by the Superintendent of Documents; a dagger (†) means distribution is by issuing agency; a phi (ɸ) indicates a publication is for sale by the Clearinghouse for Federal Scientific and Technical Information; a double dagger (‡) indicates a publication is for official use and not available to the public; and a black dot (•) indicates a publication is sent to all depository libraries which subscribe to that class of items. All those noted with an asterisk are known as GPO publications; those with other symbols as non-GPO.

Selected United States Government Publications is a biweekly annotated listing of the more popular government publications. It is available free to anyone by writing to the Superintendent of Documents and requesting to be added to the mailing list. Each issue, usually one sheet, contains an order blank for those who wish to purchase any of the documents listed.

Price Lists are booklets on many subjects which list publications available from the Superintendent of Documents. These lists are frequently revised and are available free. Each contains several order blanks. The following is a list of currently issued **Price Lists.**

10. Laws, Rules and Regulations

11. Home Economics

15. Geology

19. Army

21. Fish and Wildlife

25. Transportation, Highways, Roads and Postal Service

28. Finance

31. Education

33. Labor

33A. Occupations

35. National Parks

36. Government Periodicals and Subscription Services

37. Tariff and Taxation

38. Animal Industry

41. Insects

42. Irrigation, Drainage, and Water Power

43. Forestry

44. Plants

46. Soils and Fertilizers

48. Weather, Astronomy, and Meteorology

50. American History

51. Health and Hygiene

51A. Diseases

53. Maps

54. Political Science

55. Smithsonian Institution

58. Mines

59. Interstate Commerce

62. Commerce

63. Navy

64. Scientific Tests, Standards

65. Foreign Relations of the United States

67. Immigration, Naturalization, and Citizenship

68. Farm Management

70. Census

71. Children's Bureau

72. Homes

78. Social Security

79. Air Force

79A. Space, Missiles, the Moon, NASA, and Satellites

81. Posters and Charts

82. Radio and Electricity

83. Library of Congress

84. Atomic Energy and Civil Defense

85. Defense

86. Consumer Information

87. States and Territories of the United States and their Resources.

Publications lists are also available from many individual agencies and departments of the federal government. Publications such as **Bureau of the Census Catalog, Library of Congress Publications in Print, Publications of the Geological Survey, List of Available Publications, USDA** can be obtained by writing directly to the agency. These often list items not found in the **Monthly Catalog** or other bibliographic aids published by the Government Printing Office.

ORDERING—GENERAL PUBLICATIONS

GPO PUBLICATIONS

All publications listed in the **Price Lists, Selected United States Government Publications** and those in the **Monthly Catalog** which have an asterisk in the entry are available from the Superintendent of Documents. Sales are payable in advance in one of three ways: check or money order for the exact amount, Superintendent of Documents coupons, or by charging against a deposit account.

The general public or infrequent patron of GPO will find remitting by check or money order most convenient.

Superintendent of Documents coupons are available to anyone. They may be purchased from the Superintendent of Documents in sets of 20 for $1.00. These are especially handy for ordering inexpensive pamphlet-type documents.

A deposit account may be established by sending a check or money order for $25.00 or more to the Superintendent of Documents. An account number is then assigned and all purchases may be charged to that number.

Superintendent of Documents
Government Printing Office
Washington, D.C. 20402

The Government Printing Office also maintains eight retail bookstores which constitute a part of the operations of the Office of the Superintendent of Documents. Four are in Washington, D.C.

1. GPO Bookstore
   710 N. Capitol Street
   Washington, D.C. 20402

This was the first GPO Bookstore and was opened in 1921. It contains display space for approximately 2200 publications.

2. GPO Bookstore
   Department of Commerce—Lobby
   14th St. and Constitution Ave., N.W.
   Washington, D.C. 20230

Opened in June 1946 with space for 800-1000 publications.

3. GPO Bookstore
   USIA
   First Floor, USIA Bldg.
   1776 Pennsylvania Ave., N.W.
   Washington, D.C. 20547

   Opened in April 1947 with space for 500-700 publications.

4. GPO Bookstore
   First Floor
   Department of State Bldg.
   21st and C Streets, N.W.
   Washington, D.C. 20520

   Opened in January 1967 with space for 900 publications. This bookstore, because of limited access to the Department of State Building, is used only by employees of the Department or those visitors who are on guided tours.

Any titles published by GPO and not in stock in the above three bookstores may be ordered for pick-up the next day.

GPO Bookstores located in cities outside of Washington, D.C. will handle mail orders and all GPO publications may be ordered through any of these instead of through the Superintendent of Documents in Washington. Processing is often faster through these bookstores.

1. GPO Bookstore
   Room 1463—14th Floor
   Federal Office Bldg.
   219 S. Dearborn St.
   Chicago, III. 60604

Opened in March 1967 with space for 700 publications.

2. GPO Bookstore
   Room 135—The Federal Bldg.
   601 E. 12th Street
   Kansas City, Mo. 64106

Opened in April 1967 with space for 1000 publications. This is the first GPO Bookstore to be operated in conjunction with the Federal Information Center established by the General Services Administration (GSA).

3. GPO Bookstore
   Room 1023
   Federal Bldg.
   450 Golden Gate Avenue
   San Francisco, Calif. 94102

Space for 1000 publications.

4. GPO Bookstore
   300 No. Los Angeles St.
   Los Angeles, Calif. 90012

5. Denver, Colorado

A GPO Bookstore is scheduled to open in the Spring of 1971.

Another way to obtain GPO publications is by writing to senators or congressmen. Through the Printing Act of 1895, a certain allotment of publications is made to each senator and representative for private use or distribution. If congressmen have distribution copies of publications, they will be sent free of charge to libraries or individuals who request them.

NON-GPO PUBLICATIONS

Publications listed in the **Monthly Catalog** with a dagger by the entry and most of those listed in the various departmental or agency catalogs are known as non-GPO publications and may be obtained by writing to that issuing agency. They are usually free on request. A list of departments and agencies and their addresses is contained in Appendix B. In addition, many agencies have field offices in cities throughout the United States which may have distribution copies of publications. Persons living in cities which have agency field offices should contact those offices first.

For large libraries there are two main services for obtaining non-GPO materials in a regular or simplified manner: subscription to the Documents Expediting Project or subscription to the Readex Microprint edition of non-depository items.

The Documents Expediting Project, sponsored by the American Library Association, Association of Research Libraries, American Association of Law Libraries, and Special Libraries Association, is administered by the Library of Congress. It offers two primary services: procurement and distribution of non-GPO publications and filling special requests for out-of-print documents. Libraries pay a membership fee of from $100 to $500 a year and are entitled to services in proportion to that amount.

Documents Expediting Project
Library of Congress
Washington, D.C. 20540

The Readex Microprint Corporation makes available complete sets of non-depository items listed in the **Monthly Catalog.** There is no distribution of single publications. Instead, each non-depository publication listed in the **Monthly Catalog** is filmed in order of its appearance in the **Monthly Catalog.** The microprint copies are distributed each month and correspond to the **Monthly Catalog** entries for that month.

Readex Microprint Corp.
5 Union Square
New York, N.Y. 10003

EDUCATIONAL RESEARCH PUBLICATIONS

The Office of Education publication, **Research in Education,** announces documents resulting from federally sponsored educational research and gives cost and order number of each. This publication is available on subscription basis from the Government Printing Office.

ORDERING—EDUCATIONAL RESEARCH PUBLICATIONS

The documents listed in **Research in Education** are available from the Educational Research Information Center (ERIC), a nationwide information network consisting of a central staff and many clearinghouses. Each clearing-house specializes in a particular field of educational research. Publications should be ordered from:

ERIC Document Reproduction Service
National Cash Register Company
Box 2206
Rockville, Md. 20852

SCIENTIFIC AND TECHNICAL PUBLICATIONS

Three major current sources of federal government scientific and technical information are **U.S. Government Research and Development Reports (USGRDR), Technical Abstract Bulletin (TAB),** and **Scientific and Technical Aerospace Reports (STAR).**

USGRDR is a biweekly listing of unclassified and unrestricted technical reports of the Defense Documentation Center (DDC), National Aeronautics and Space Administration (NASA), Atomic Energy Commission (AEC) and many other federal departments and agencies. The publications listed in **USGRDR** are available from the Clearinghouse for Federal Scientific and Technical Information (CFSTI) and cover the following areas:

1. Aeronautics
2. Agriculture
3. Astronomy & Astrophysics
4. Atmospheric Sciences
5. Behavioral and Social Sciences
6. Biological and Medical Sciences
7. Chemistry
8. Earth Sciences and Oceanography
9. Electronics and Electrical Engineering
10. Energy Conversion
11. Materials

12. Mathematical Sciences

13. Mechanical, Industrial, Civil and Marine Engineering

14. Methods and Equipment

15. Military Sciences

16. Missile Technology

17. Navigation, Communications, Detection, and Countermeasures

18. Nuclear Science and Technology

19. Ordnance

20. Physics

21. Propulsion and Fuels

22. Space Technology

TAB is a semi-monthly abstract journal listing publications from the DDC which are restricted or limited in distribution. It is provided for use by qualified patrons of the DDC.

STAR is a semi-monthly abstract journal published by NASA listing scientific and technical reports of NASA, government agencies, research centers and universities throughout the world. There are thirty-four major subject areas covered by **STAR** including aerodynamics, biosciences, computers, electronics, geophysics, masers, navigation, propulsion systems, thermodynamics and combustion.

ORDERING—SCIENTIFIC AND TECHNICAL PUBLICATIONS

Publications listed in **USGRDR** are available from the Clearinghouse for Federal Scientific and Technical Information in one of two forms. Microfiche copies of documents cost $0.65 and paper copies are $3.00. Like GPO, CFSTI publications may be purchased by check or money order, prepaid document coupon (in denominations of either $3.00 or $0.65) or by charging against a deposit account (established with a minimum deposit of $25.00).

Clearinghouse for Federal Scientific and Technical Information
Springfield, Va. 22151

Department of Defense documents and contractor reports listed in **TAB** are classified or limited in distribution. Eligible persons may obtain documents by writing:

Defense Documentation Center
Attn: DDC-L
Cameron Station
Alexandria, Va. 22314

STAR lists documents available from CFSTI, GPO and NASA, with source noted for each publication. Follow procedures already listed for ordering from GPO or CFSTI. To order from NASA use the following address:

National Aeronautics & Space Administration
Scientific & Technical Information Facility
P. O. Box 33
College Park, Md. 20740

APPENDIX B

DIRECTORY OF ISSUING AGENCIES

Agriculture Department
Washington, D.C. 20250

Agricultural Marketing Service
Department of Agriculture
Washington, D.C. 20250

Agricultural Research Service
Department of Agriculture
Washington, D.C. 20250

Agricultural Stabilization and Conservation
 Service
Department of Agriculture
Washington, D.C. 20250

Air Force Department
Department of Defense
Washington, D.C. 20330

Armed Forces Information Service
Department of Defense
Washington, D.C. 20301

Arms Control and Disarmament Agency
Washington, D.C. 20451

Army Department
Department of Defense
Washington, D.C. 20310

Atomic Energy Commission
Washington, D.C. 20545

Business and Defense Services Administration
Department of Commerce
Washington, D.C. 20230

Business Economics Office
Department of Commerce
Washington, D.C. 20230

Coast and Geodetic Survey
Department of Commerce
Washington, D.C. 20230

Coast Guard
Department of the Treasury
Washington, D.C. 20591

Census Bureau
Department of Commerce
Suitland, Md. 20233

Children's Bureau
Department of Health, Education and Welfare
Washington, D.C. 20201

Civil Defense Office
Department of Defense
Washington, D.C. 20310

Civil Rights Commission
Washington, D.C. 20425

Civil Service Commission
Washington, D.C. 20415

Clearinghouse for Federal Scientific and
  Technical Information
Springfield, Va. 22151

Commerce Department
Washington, D.C. 20230

Commercial Fisheries Bureau
Department of the Interior
Washington, D.C. 20240

Consumer and Marketing Service
Department of Agriculture
Washington, D.C. 20250

Cooperative State Research Service
Department of Agriculture
Washington, D.C. 20250

Copyright Office
Library of Congress
Washington, D.C. 20540

Defense Department
Washington, D.C. 20301

Economic Development Administration
Department of Commerce
Washington, D.C. 20230

Economic Opportunity Office
Executive Office of the President
Washington, D.C. 20506

Economic Research Service
Department of Agriculture
Washington, D.C. 20250

Education Office
Department of Health, Education and Welfare
Washington, D.C. 20202

Employment Security Bureau
Department of Labor
Washington, D.C. 20210

Environmental Science Services Administration
Department of Commerce
Washington, D.C. 20235

Federal Aviation Administration
Department of Transportation
Washington, D.C. 20553

Federal Communications Commission
Washington, D.C. 20554

Federal Council for Science and Technology
Washington, D.C. 20506

Federal Highway Administration
Department of Transportation
Washington, D.C. 20591

Federal Home Loan Bank Board
Washington, D.C. 20552

Federal Power Commission
Washington, D.C. 20426

Federal Reserve System
Washington, D.C. 20551

Federal Water Pollution Control Administration
Department of the Interior
Washington, D.C. 20242

Fish and Wildlife Service
Department of the Interior
Washington, D.C. 20240

Food and Drug Administration
Department of Health, Education and Welfare
Washington, D.C. 20201

Foreign Agricultural Service
Department of Agriculture
Washington, D.C. 20250

Foreign Broadcast Information Service
Executive Office of the President
Washington, D.C. 20506

Forest Service
Department of Agriculture
Washington, D.C. 20250

General Accounting Office
Washington, D.C. 20548

General Services Administration
Washington, D.C. 20405

Geological Survey
Department of the Interior
Washington, D.C. 20405

Health, Education and Welfare Department
Washington, D.C. 20201

House of Representatives
Washington, D.C. 20515

Immigration and Naturalization Service
Department of Justice
Washington, D.C. 20536

Indian Affairs Bureau
Department of the Interior
Washington, D.C. 20240

Interagency Committee on Mexican American
 Affairs
1800 G Street, N.W.
Washington, D.C. 20506

Interior Department
Washington, D.C. 20240

Internal Revenue Service
Department of the Treasury
Washington, D.C. 20224

International Commerce Bureau
Department of Commerce
Washington, D.C. 20230

International Development Agency
Department of State
Washington, D.C. 20523

International Labor Affairs Bureau
Department of Labor
Washington, D.C. 20210

Joint Chiefs of Staff
Department of Defense
Washington, D.C. 20301

Justice Department
Washington, D.C. 20530

Labor Department
Washington, D.C. 20210

Labor Standards Bureau
Department of Labor
Washington, D.C. 20210

Labor Statistics Bureau
Department of Labor
Washington, D.C. 20210

Land Management Bureau
Department of the Interior
Washington, D.C. 20240

Library of Congress
Washington, D.C. 20540

Marine Corps
Department of Defense
Washington, D.C. 20350

Maritime Administration
Department of Commerce
Washington, D.C. 20548

Military History Office
Department of Defense
Washington, D.C. 20310

Mines Bureau
Department of the Interior
Washington, D.C. 20240

National Agricultural Library
Department of Agriculture
Washington, D.C. 20250

National Aeronautics & Space Administration
Washington, D.C. 20546

National Archives and Records Service
General Services Administration
Washington, D.C. 20408

National Bureau of Standards
Department of Commerce
Gaithersburg, Md. 20760

National Center for Social Statistics
Department of Health, Education and Welfare
Washington, D.C. 20201

National Clearinghouse for Mental Health
  Information
National Institute of Mental Health
Department of Health, Education and Welfare
Chevy Chase, Md. 20015

National Collection of Fine Arts
Smithsonian Institution
Washington, D.C. 20560

National Endowment for the Arts
National Foundation on the Arts and Humanities
Washington, D.C. 20506

National Endowment for the Humanities
National Foundation on the Arts and Humanities
Washington, D.C. 20506

National Foundation on the Arts and Humanities
Washington, D.C. 20506

National Gallery of Art
Smithsonian Institution
Washington, D.C. 20560

National Highway Safety Bureau
Department of Transportation
Washington, D.C. 20591

National Historical Publications Committee
Smithsonian Institution
Washington, D.C. 20560

National Institute of Mental Health
Department of Health, Education and Welfare
Chevy Chase, Md. 20015

National Institutes of Health
Department of Health, Education and Welfare
Bethesda, Md. 20014

National Labor Relations Board
Washington, D.C. 20570

National Museum
Smithsonian Institution
Washington, D.C. 20560

National Park Service
Department of the Interior
Washington, D.C. 20240

National Portrait Gallery
Smithsonian Institution
Washington, D.C. 20560

National Science Foundation
Washington, D.C. 20550

Naval Oceanographic Office
Department of Defense
Washington, D.C. 20390

Naval Operations Office
Department of Defense
Washington, D.C. 20390

Naval Research Office
Department of Defense
Washington, D.C. 20390

Navy Department
Department of Defense
Washington, D.C. 20390

Outdoor Recreation Bureau
Department of the Interior
Washington, D.C. 20240

Patent Office
Department of Commerce
Washington, D.C. 20231

Peace Corps
Department of State
Washington, D.C. 20525

Post Office Department
Washington, D.C. 20260

President of the United States
Washington, D.C. 20501

Public Documents Division
Government Printing Office
Washington, D.C. 20402

Public Health Service
Department of Health, Education and Welfare
Washington, D.C. 20201

Public Roads Bureau
Department of Transportation
Washington, D.C. 20591

Reclamation Bureau
Department of the Interior
Washington, D.C. 20240

Rehabilitation Service
Department of Health, Education and Welfare
Washington, D.C. 20201

Rural Community Development Service
Department of Agriculture
Washington, D.C. 20250

Rural Electrification Administration
Department of Agriculture
Washington, D.C. 20250

Securities and Exchange Commission
Washington, D.C. 20549

Senate
Washington, D.C. 20510

Small Business Administration
Washington, D.C. 20416

Smithsonian Institution
Washington, D.C. 20560

Social & Rehabilitation Service
Department of Health, Education and Welfare
Washington, D.C. 20201

Social Security Administration
Department of Health, Education and Welfare
Washington, D.C. 20201

Soil Conservation Service
Department of Agriculture
Washington, D.C. 20250

Sport Fisheries and Wildlife Bureau
Department of the Interior
Washington, D.C. 20240

State Department
Washington, D.C. 20520

Statistical Reporting Service
Department of Agriculture
Washington, D.C. 20250

Superintendent of Documents
Government Printing Office
Washington, D.C. 20402

Tennessee Valley Authority
Washigton, D.C. 20444

Transportation Department
Washington, D.C. 20591

Travel Service
Department of Commerce
Washington, D.C. 20230

Treasury Department
Washington, D.C. 20220

U.S. Military Academy
Department of Defense
West Point, N. Y. 10996

U.S. Travel Service
Department of Commerce
Washington, D.C. 20230

Veteran's Administration
Washington, D.C. 20420

Volunteers in Service to America (VISTA)
Executive Office of the President
Washington, D.C. 20506

Women's Bureau
Department of Labor
Washington, D.C. 20210

INDEX

Children and Poetry: A Selective Annotated Bibliography, 21
Children's Books, 1968, A List of Books for Preschool Through Junior High School Age, 22
Children's Bureau, 66, 72, 90-91, 96, 369, 492, 522
Children's Bureau publications lists, 90
Chilman, Catherine S., 75
Ciompi, L., 509
Civil Defense Office, 484-86
Civil Defense Office publications lists, 485
Civil rights, 98-99
Civil Rights Commission, 98-99
Civil Rights Commission publications lists, 98
Civil Rights Directory, 99
Civil Service Commission, 238, 275, 277-79, 289
Civil service employment, 116, 275, 277-79, 289, 363-64, 388
Civil War, 154
Clare, Kenneth G., 168
Clark, William Bell, 129
Clavichords, 595
Cleft lip and cleft palate services, 501
Climate of Cities: A Survey of Recent Literature, 452
Climates of the World, 449
Climatic Atlas of the United States, 450
Climatology, 448-452
Cloud, William K., 463
Coast and Geodetic Survey, 459-60, 462-63
Coast Guard, 225
Coffman, Jerry L., 463
Cold Storage Warehouses Freezing and Storing Fishery Products, 220

College Student Volunteers in State Mental Hospitals, 533
Colleges and Universities, 35, 37, 43, 76, 108
Commerce Department, 194, 200-02, 425
Commerce Department publications lists, 201-02
Commercial Fisheries Bureau, 220, 410, 419, 420
Commonwealth of Nations, 114
Communications, 63-65, 467
Communications-Electronics Terminology, 467
Community Health Service Publications Catalog, 545
Community mental health centers, 526, 528-29
Community Property and the Federal Income Tax, 353
Compendium of State Statutes on the Regulation of Ambulance Services, Operation of Emergency Vehicles and Good Samaritan Laws, 556
Compensatory education, 52
Comprehensive Community Mental Health Center: An Annotated Bibliography, 525
Comprehensive Health Planning: A Selected Annotated Bibliography, 546
Computers, 425, 507
Computers, Selected Bibliographic Citations Announced in U.S. Government Research and Development Reports, 425
Computing Your Tax Under the Income Averaging Method, 304
Condemnations of Private Property for Public Use, 347
Condon, Patricia A., 559
Confederate States of America, 156
Congress, 97, 119-20

189

194